Waking Up to This Day

Waking Up to This Day

for Denise —

Seeing the Beauty Right before Us

Life itself is the great gift —
Paula D'Arcy

Paula D'Arcy

ORBIS BOOKS

Maryknoll, New York 10545

Founded in 1970, Orbis Books endeavors to publish works that enlighten the mind, nourish the spirit, and challenge the conscience. The publishing arm of the Maryknoll Fathers and Brothers, Orbis seeks to explore the global dimensions of the Christian faith and mission, to invite dialogue with diverse cultures and religious traditions, and to serve the cause of reconciliation and peace. The books published reflect the views of their authors and do not represent the official position of the Maryknoll Society. To learn more about Maryknoll and Orbis Books, please visit our website at www.maryknollsociety.org.

Library of Congress Cataloging-in-Publication Data

D'Arcy, Paula, 1947-
    Waking up to this day : seeing the beauty right before us / Paula D'Arcy.
        p. cm.
    ISBN 978-1-57075-849-2 (pbk.)
    1. Christian life.   2. Awareness—Religious aspects—Christianity.
I. Title.
    BV4501.3.D37 2009
    248.2—dc22
                                                            2009018709

for Connie Barrios
(1957-2009)

Contents

Preface

This is a book about waking up to the day that is right before us—about meeting each moment as it is. It is designed for those of us who are ready to experience a deeper intimacy with ourselves, with others, and with all that is. At the heart of these pages is the belief that as we awaken to our deepest self, we stop relating to life and to others primarily through expectation or through mind activity. Instead, we begin to meet each person, place, or thing directly. We wake up to this day.

These chapters emphasize the power of being present to each moment. Charles Stanford writes, "Heaven must be in me before I can be in heaven." I hope you will come to know that wisdom. Awakening is not a concept or a set of holy conditions to attain. It is the direct experience of spirit in life and our full response to that presence. As a woman in a seminar recently observed, "It's as if spirit whispers to us, 'Uncover me.'"

Within these chapters are stories from my own journey. I'm sharing them with you in the hope that my discoveries will encourage your own exploration. The stories reveal that there is no single, universal experience that defines awakening. Sometimes a simple, everyday moment is the gateway to wonder.

I have outlined nine keys that have been guideposts for

me. Each key is a continuing summons to live in the present moment and to accept the perfection of life as it unfolds. The keys teach us that life is right here, right now. They reveal the beauty of life just as it is. It is my hope that you will learn, as I am learning, to see the day before you with new eyes. Beneath the superficial appearance of things lies a deeper force and a greater purpose—life's own intrinsic meaning.

I encourage you to be reflective at the end of each chapter. Walk outside and let the natural world guide you. The wisdom of Nature has been there all along, inviting us to move past our conditioning and even our darkness—waiting for us to meet each thing with love.

Acknowledgments

*W*ith deep gratitude to my editor, Mike Leach, for his seasoned and considerable wisdom and guidance. He looked at my initial, tattered notes and assured me it could work.

With inexpressible thanks to the many friends in Alaska who took the time to show me the beauty that surrounds them each day, especially Don Darnell, and also Diana Conroy, Jan and Jim Thurston (who own and operate the incomparable Stillpoint Lodge in Halibut Cove), and Wellyngton.

To the Dull Men's club of Halibut Cove, Alaska (you know who you are, Don, George, and Steve) for the gift of deep laughter and unmitigated joy.

My great appreciation to Pam Tomlinson and Flint Sparks for providing their own writers' ears, eyes, and hearts to my ongoing process, and for helping me immeasurably in that way—and even more so as friends.

My gratitude to Robin Ridder for providing a place of respite and beauty for me during a year with heavy travel and the press of writing deadlines. Her meals alone could make anyone prolific.

And the greatest thanks, always, to my daughter Beth, who is my buffer as I write, holding off the phone calls, responding to the e-mails, and allowing me to take the time and space that bringing a book to life requires—all without complaint.

Waking Up to This Day

Introduction

In 1975 I survived an automobile accident that took the lives of my young husband and daughter. Six months later, still in the wake of that storm, I gave birth to a second daughter, Beth. Finding my way through the grief gave rise to a long period of healing. During that time my love for writing was an anchor and a harbor. Writing moved the pain, my pen pushing at fear and confusion like a plow opening a path through the snow. In that cleared space I eventually found hope and a way to go on.

My eyes opened to the simplicity and power in the ordinary moments of daily living, and I was deeply stirred by the lessons life has to offer. I began to notice how much time and attention I gave to things that really didn't matter. Like everyone else, I got caught up in the busyness and details of work. Joan Chittister writes, "You get credentialed in something . . . you have a career, a profession, a skill, a piece of the world on which to mark your presence . . . We 'go along' in life rather than living." I had "gone along" without even being aware that there was a different way to be.

Nearly fifteen years later, in 1989, I took a step toward "living." That spring I ventured into a beautiful wilderness area in

1

the Southwest to make a vision quest, a story I tell in my book *Gift of the Red Bird*. This three-day fast in the solitude of the natural world became an experience of great importance for me. In retrospect, I was wholly unprepared for what I would meet. And it *was* a meeting. I was met by a presence whose love spoke directly to my deepest heart.

This experience was powerful and challenged many of my opinions and points of view about life. The challenges came via a storm that arose in the desert, and through hunger, heat, fatigue, fear—and finally by a red bird that frequented the place where I sat and offered not only companionship but my first experience of the responsiveness of all creation.

The distinction between "going along" in life and conscious "living" was never clearer, and the impact of my initial meeting with Nature has been lasting. My former conclusions about life sounded good and important as theory or philosophy; in the wilderness they were lacking in countless ways.

"I beseech you," says Oliver Cromwell, "think it possible you may be mistaken." That one line became light for me. It was clear that I had not yet developed past the unexamined conclusions I'd drawn in my earliest years. I'd lived as if I had life figured out. The sudden death of my family, plus those days and nights alone in Nature, proved to me that I knew very little.

Now I was challenged to grow up. I could see that the gift of life was unequaled. The question was, would I live it? Would I let the spirit within and not my opinions and former knowledge take me the rest of the way? This deeper faith was the intimate call of a real presence, not a matter of better beliefs or improved theology. It demanded a marked change in the way I related to everything around me.

I glimpsed a freedom that could be mine. I didn't have to remain who I'd always been or repeat choices that didn't work for me. I could begin anew, seeing life without the continuous overlay of judgment and expectation. The past and its deeply ingrained patterns and traditions did not have to be my primary perspective. Those conclusions weren't a final truth—they were just one way of looking. I sensed what a journey under the guidance of soul might be. The spirit embedded in the ordinary moments of life became my light.

"Are you brave enough to awaken?" a teacher asked me, looking straight into my eyes. It was the right question. It still is.

All of us must ultimately find our own way. Still, there are guideposts, small glimmers of light, like a circle of elders, which direct all journeys. These markers set us squarely in front of the present moment and summon us to grow up into a full maturity.

It became increasing insignificant whether or not my life experiences were momentarily favorable or unfavorable. Spirit moves in each thing, a deep knowledge laboring tirelessly on our behalf, willing us to recognize the difference between the life we're living and the life that wants to be known and lived in us. We are here for so much more than we realize.

In the end, the goal does not rest on being successful or even happy. It's about finding a way through the layers of resistance that keep us frightened and small. Waking up to our deepest nature, we see life as it is and ourselves as we truly are. We finally see what's possible.

As I struggled to integrate new awareness into my life I made many missteps and frequently reverted to former patterns of thinking. I still held tightly to old, familiar beliefs. I took three steps forward, two steps back and lost my way more than once. I saw my resistance to the life being held out to me and my keen determination to keep things comfortable and unchanging. Rising up to meet the life force on its own terms demanded complete acquiescence.

Plato speaks of figures sitting in a cave facing forward, mesmerized by the shadows cast on the wall in front of them—shadows that appear to be real. Yet it is the one casting the shadow who is real, and the figures have only to turn around and look in that direction. In turning, the error of misperception is corrected. Waking up is like that. The turning allows a direct experience of spirit in life. Awakened to this, we begin to realize that within every circumstance is a hidden power that runs from the depths to the surface.

In the following pages I have remained faithful to the markers that guided my journey but I have not always related life events in their chronological order. The stories are told when and as they serve the thread being woven through the work. They are photos from my life that reveal moments when light made the picture come alive. I share them in the hopes that through them your own life will become more transparent.

I travel the world sharing how the initial loss of my family was the seed for so much insight. To make this picture complete I return briefly to that beginning and ask those readers who know this piece of my journey to bear with the repetition. The text also includes many stories written from Alaska where I recently spent several weeks over a period of two years. Its unspoiled beauty affected me deeply.

Awakening to the present moment—to now—is to look without a filter. We bridge the great divide between our individual perception of life and life as it is. All words are inadequate before the gift. The path is simply waking up to this very moment. The same presence that I met on my quest for vision speaks to every human heart.

—Paula D'Arcy, April 2009

You don't even need to leave your room.
Remain sitting at your table and listen.
Don't even listen, simply wait.
Don't even wait, be still and solitary.
The world will freely offer itself to you
to be unmasked. It has no choice.
It will roll in ecstasy at your feet.

                              —Franz Kafka

1

Decide What Really Matters

I was a young woman in 1975—glad, confident, in love— when profound loss entered my world with its serrated edges. Twenty-seven years old, an accident, a driver reeling with liquor flying across a divided interstate to find his innocent mark. My husband and young daughter both fell to his blow. That speeding car, careening through the air, realigned my every priority within seconds. I was three months pregnant, alive, shattered, and eye to eye with a force I could not identify. It overpowered everything, like a heavy cloak thrown down to smother a fire.

Nothing else mattered then. Not my education, my training, my modest successes. They were a pitiful match for the hand flinging my world into a new mold. I became a scavenger, picking my way through the debris, hunting for pieces of broken dreams. But the splinters on the edge of my dreams were too fragile and irregular to glue back together. There was only the option to start fresh. Now I could see how much their lives had mattered. Everything else was expendable. Life was the gift all along.

I shouldered the pain and searched for a way to re-establish even a glimmer of hope. Who was I, before the searing sadness? What was important to me then? What had I paid attention to?

I was the woman putting things off. *I'll do this later. We'll do it next year.* Next year. Who could believe that the years would run out, young as we were? But they did run out, runaway horses galloping at high speed, the whole length of the reins streaming behind them. There was no next year. It came down to something that simple. There had never been a guarantee.

I watched my hands as if they held answers. What was I holding onto?

What was important? Very few things, the hands told me. Very few. The words spoken by my hands would not leave me.

Grief tore through me like a virus, no cell left untouched. My cousin and his wife also lost a child at the same time . . . a son. We sat together one evening, huddled around the charred remains of our lives like old cowboys tending a fire that had once blazed but was now reduced to scraps of soft, burning coals. I ran my hand over the arm of my cousin's living room chair. Our eyes were deep, dark hollows. A stray thread hung from my maternity top and I wound and unwound it around my little finger. I picked at the thread in rhythm with the ticking of my watch. And we sat there in the lamplight, dizzy from the effort to breathe against blinding pain.

It was as if a wall of water surrounded the room, pressing with force on all sides against our breaking hearts. With or without a name, the pain was upending everything I knew.

It pushed its way into us that comfortless night. And what I couldn't see, and wouldn't see for years, was the freedom in its wake. For the first time in my life I was not persuaded by the false importance of a single thing. The knot that had tethered me to illusive shadows had been cut, and in its place was an interior clarity worth possessing. An early light. Grief's single question, What really matters? illuminated a great dark. Few things really matter, and those that do, matter dearly. Establishing what really matters is the first step.

The question of what matters began to push against me. It was a searchlight moving across my biography with a revealing glare. It exposed my everyday choices and showed me that no matter what I said, I was not fully committed to the values I professed. The truth was that I lived trying not to rock the boat. I was devoted to keeping things stable, reducing any threat that the familiar structures of my life would shift. It did not occur to me that change, the shifting of things, was essential to life. In fact, was life.

Questions about what really matters intensified. Losing my family was an obvious, life-changing experience, but there were other instances when the question of what really matters was more subtle and mundane. Over the years, for example, I spent treasured summer days at a small cottage on the Connecticut shore. My intention was always to relax, but even more so, to reconnect with the sea. There is no spot on earth closer to my bone. Yet I frequently arrived at that cottage door with my arms full: books to read, writing to finish, household chores to accomplish while there, screens to wash, cupboards to clean and rearrange. I arrived at the place I valued the most carrying a To Do list that guaranteed I would hear and experience very little. I was wed to my agenda. Sometimes a week or two passed before I looked at myself and saw what I was doing. Then the question of what really matters would reemerge.

I learned to slow down and spend time in Nature, nurturing the connection that brings me back to myself. As long as I was rushing and checking items off a To Do list, I continued to live in my mind and not in the present moment. Ordinary moments brought me back to Earth's beauty: The sun setting over the water in front of the beach cottage, a small arc of reddish light coloring the sand . . . The deeper part of me, my hidden nature, found its sustenance in the lowering light at dusk and the smell of seaweed and salt at dawn. I calmed down. It was possible to meet life directly—I simply had to be present.

The pilgrim-poet Basho calls such moments a "glimpse of the underglimmer." The word is fanciful but the reality to which it points is not frivolous. A glimpse of the underglimmer is nourishment for the deeper self. It's the light of awareness piercing the apparent dark.

By getting closer to the stretch of sand and water before me, even by immersing myself in barnacles and slow tides, I found my way back home. For a few days the louder, competing voices of the culture were mercifully silenced. I would return soon enough to a fuller pace. But in that brief walking away—within that margin—Nature's presence touched me. Her knowledge is simple and direct: hidden in the busyness of everyday life is Life. But you have to turn toward it. Otherwise, we live in our minds, identified with mind activity, and are endlessly caught in what Joko Beck describes as "the self-centered dream."

On another occasion I gathered with friends in Alabama for the unexpected and heart-rending funeral of a young man who had died tragically in an accident. We were all bent double with grief, numbly watching the large numbers of family and friends who came to offer comfort. I wrote in my journal, *This is what it is to bear the details of your life.* As we sat huddled together on the following day, my friend Eric asked the question, "Why don't we feel the same urgency to move heaven and earth to be together for life, and not just death?" I could not let his words go.

They reminded me of the movie *Snow Walker*, where a native woman starts a fire by blowing on embers that are held within a circle of moss. She heaves like a bellows until her breath ignites the grasses. All that matters is starting that fire. Without the fire, her life and the life of the man with whom she is traveling in the North Country will be ended. Her ability to meet that moment saves them both. She discerns what really matters and rises to meet the power in that challenge with equal presence. The force of her clarity is enviable. She immediately knew what mattered because, in this instance, the situation was desperate. But could she (I?) have breathed life into the embers as forcefully without the pressing danger? What does it take to bring everything we have to bear on moments that are less commanding and more ordinary? "Our true life," observes Joko Beck, "[can] go by almost unnoticed."

In the months before his death, esteemed psychologist and author Gerald May describes a moment of his own awakening.

He has made repeated trips to the wilderness while dealing with the effects of advancing cancer and impending death. During that period, he experiences a growing awareness of the night and the mystery of the forest. One evening as he approaches the woods he says to the forest, "I want to be taken in." I read that sentence and stopped reading any further.

So much meaning is held in his words. They bear witness to his intimacy with himself and to all that is, as well as his acquiescence to the lymphoma that, in the end, was not arrested. "Wilderness is not just a place," he concludes. "It is also a state of being . . . it's the untamed truth of who you really are."

Gerald May learned to stand before that truth and ask questions: What is life trying to teach me? What wants to be known? His will to grow pushed him past "the self-centered dream" into a different experience. In the end he saw the limitations of the mind's relentless activity—all the concepts that masquerade as reality. Now he knew differently: Life can be experienced directly. What appears to be hidden can be known. When the distractions and misperceptions fell away, he was face to face with right now. His deepest self responded with the words, *Take me in.*

In his book, *Three Cups of Tea*, Greg Mortenson tells the story of a similar moment when he too was directly confronted by the power and immediacy of now. In that moment he shifted from living within his "thoughts about things" to a direct encounter with the world that had always been right before him.

An avid mountain climber, he had just failed an attempt to summit K2, one of the highest and most challenging peaks in the world, set in the high mountains of northern Pakistan. During this particular climb, weakened by physical demands on his body because of the high altitude, and also weakened by his rescue of a fellow climber at considerable danger to himself, Greg realizes that he cannot continue. He slowly makes his way back down the mountain, deeply disheartened. He ultimately loses his way, becomes separated from his trail guide, and is unable to get his bearings. He spends a long night shivering in the bitter cold. Then as the sun comes up, he stops to look at the view before him.

"He stood at the top of a crest just as the rising sun climbed free of the valley walls. It was as if he'd been shot through the eyes. The panorama blinded him . . . Though he had already been there for months, he drank in the drama of these peaks like he'd never seen them before.

" 'In a way, I never had,' he explains. 'All summer, I'd looked at these mountains as goals, totally focused on the biggest one, K2. I'd thought about their elevation and the technical challenges they presented to me as a climber. But that morning,' he says, 'for the first time, I simply saw them. It was overwhelming.' "

Whether the moment of new awareness is provoked by an experience of sadness or fullness, the pattern is still the same. We are suddenly aware of an unexplainable power and are taken over by the realization that nothing else matters, because nothing else is real. The past is memory and the future is a thought. Only the present can be met. The familiar grip of mind and thought is momentarily loosened, and something else is glimpsed. Life creates an opening.

A friend from Alaska describes such an experience at sea. "I was alone on the bridge wing in the afternoon, watching the water. Watching, and watching. Just watching the water go by. Witnessing. Noticing the different currents and how they meet, the upwelling, the rips, the places where the birds feed, and why. It's the water, this moving *through* the water, and then, [suddenly] this water moving through me."

In that break from thinking "about" things, something indescribable arises that transcends ordinary knowledge. Everything comes alive. Thinking about things cannot compare to this power. Thoughts produce wanting, not fullness—they produce self-centeredness, not vision—they serve as distractions, not a means of clarifying sight. In the experience of waking up to what is right before us, there is no sense of "me" or "mine," no mental thoughts and beliefs. Everything else falls away and you find yourself looking at life without judgment or interpretation. You simply see.

Once, while driving through Utah in the late afternoon on a cross-country trip with my daughter, Beth, I experienced that same forceful break from the mind's hold. We were on an isolated stretch of road and were caught by a sudden, strong storm with its thundering streaks of lightning and lashing rain. The slippery road ahead was barely visible. Even on a clear, dry day the roadway's deep pattern of switchbacks was challenging, but in the growing dark the invisible drop-offs were frightening. We'd been traveling for hours without seeing another car. We had no cell phone coverage and no idea how much further we had to travel before reaching people and shelter. I'd never felt so far into the embrace of night.

Beth's voice broke into the darkness. "Right now," she whispered, "no one in the world knows where we are. If something happens, we won't be found." And frightening as that felt, it was also deeply and strangely enlivening. The normal fracture between Nature and human life had been bridged. I realized that I was no longer looking *at* rain and lightning. We were *in* the storm, and that immediacy produced a startling connection with Nature, as well as a visceral awareness of her power.

At that moment, nothing else mattered. We were fully present. We were the storm, and the mountains we couldn't see . . . the drop-offs beneath us. I was aware of being fully and profoundly alive. With physical vision limited and darkness falling, something else arose—a largeness and brilliance that is just beneath ordinary awareness. I was aware of nothing beyond my daughter's presence in the seat beside me, the storm, and the night. Fright fell away, replaced by an unusual peace. Though the circumstances were still dangerous, a sense of aliveness and well-being prevailed.

That moment is one of a growing handful of experiences when I have been fully present to the life before me. That night, even as my eyes continued to search the dark to find the white guide lines painted on the road, fear and danger no longer had the power to unsettle me. There was only my growing sense that the mountains I couldn't see not only knew that we were there but were, in fact, watching. I saw that we were of the same essence—only our substance was different. In Gerald May's words, I had been "taken in." I sensed an undeniable and intimate connection between the world of Nature and the deeper nature that was opening within me. There was, in fact, no difference between them—only the illusion of separation created by the mind. Catherine of Siena writes, "My deepest me is God."

On another occasion I was traveling with a group of women in Alaska. We were in a small boat, grey waves parting at the bow, when I saw the first plume of spray. It took several seconds for me to understand what that meant, and by then one of the women was already shouting to the others, "Whales!" The first sleek, lumbering humpback lifted slowly from the frigid waters like a single streak of grace. Back arched, his rubbery tonnage rose into the air, showers of spray spitting back onto the sea. I couldn't breathe. Then, just as gracefully, he lowered himself back into the brine, his tail fanned with the flourish of royalty. We never moved. It was a flower opening, a split in the ordinariness of things, that single tail lifting and offering itself to the morning. Then slowly, with elegance, the great tail slunk down and was repossessed by the water. As the tail slipped from sight the second whale was already rising. I kept hearing my voice. *Oh my God, oh my God. My God.* We were all screaming, the six of us, the great gift of the whales too enormous to take in silently. We had to make sound.

Our boat slowed until we were thirty feet away. We rocked

gently in the water, watching. There were three of them. We heard the great shush of spray, followed by the enormity of their leaping. One after the other, rhythmically, they bounded from the deep. My mind was not possessed by a single thought. Nothing. Everything was the rise and fall of the whales.

We'd called to them as we set out that morning. I was staying on, but for the other women it was their last day in Alaska. They were on their way to Anchorage and the planes that would take them home. *Please, show yourselves, we'd each silently intoned. Come.* Life calling life, with nothing else intervening. And they came.

It felt as if a mighty hand had put the whales in a bow and shot them into the thickness of our collective dream state, willing us to see. The mark of the arrow was true. It wasn't just the whales and their beautifulness . . . their leaping. In fact, it wasn't nearly that. It was the power that brings whales into being and the will of that power to know us. It was God putting God into a bow in the form of a whale, responding to our silent plea, *Come.*

The moment struck a universal marrow, speaking a language I dimly understood. The whales were voices arising from a fertile soil where the deepest knowledge lies, waiting. They shouted to us, Don't go back to sleep. This fullness is meant for you.

It's as if each of us has another, deeper life than the one being lived. It lies underneath our ordinary days, our errands, the doing of dishes, the writing of letters, the making of money, like something moving, lobsterlike, under water. This only partially understood life (refused, often; banished, easily ignored) might be

*what we call the soul. The desire to know about it causes us to
pray. But all the while, it's moving toward something, as surely as
we are advancing in our lives, through careers, marriage, children.
Every now and then this hidden life surfaces . . . like a glimpse
of things in that peculiar, vivid light after a rain.*

—Nora Gallagher, *Changing Light*

One evening in Alaska friends offered to bring me to my
cabin in their skiff. A full moon lit the water. I stepped from
the dock into the boat and we began to motor away. I was sitting alone at the back of the boat and my eye looked out over
the sea. I knew very well that we were gliding on the water's
surface, creating small furrows of wake as we passed. But the
vivid moonlight created a looking glass effect, casting brilliant
reflections of moon, clouds, and mountain into the water until
the water's surface appeared to be many feet below where it
actually was. It created a feeling of complete disequilibrium,
and I couldn't shake the sense that we were sinking down . . .
that the thin surface of the water was not where it should be,
nor would it hold us. No matter how I tried to think otherwise,
my mind bedeviled me with the image that we were about to
drop into the sea.

It was both momentarily frightening and also beguiling.
It felt as if we were suspended—floating, unattached—held
in place only by a mysterious pull beyond my mental grasp. I
thought of the doorway leading out to the sea in the famous
Edward Hopper painting. Now I was viscerally experiencing
the disquiet of that threshold. I finally reoriented myself by
looking up at the sky.

The experience was forceful. For a moment gravity appeared to be suspended; the usual heaviness and density of thought was lifted as well. I was fully present to my surroundings, conscious of nothing else, and nothing else intruded. There was only the boat, the sea, and the night.

As the boat slid through the heart of the water it opened a different awareness. In its wake the beauty and power of life was palpable. Everything was present—the ordinariness of life, and then a greater life lying underneath the surface. Later, lying in bed, images of that boat ride pushed against me like waves against my skin. I heard the words, Do not squander this gift. Do not squander your life.

Nature continues to open doorways that are more than doorways. She takes us by the hand and stands us before the experiences that are waiting for us—the animals, the oceans, the views, the glimpses of light on water, the underglimmer. Toni Morrison lends her own understanding when she writes, "I'm just trying to look at something without blinking." And, it seems, in this twenty-first century of continuing violence and unrest, that our future depends upon our being able to look without blinking. It depends upon our waking to the deeper life that moves in life, the life that sustains being. It depends upon our knowing what really matters and living out of that knowledge. It depends upon our opening to this deeper nature and being able to sustain a small glimpse of the "peculiar, vivid light after a rain."

When we see something as it is, the breaking of the shell begins. My friend Flint reflects, "Even to look at an iris and think, 'Such a beautiful flower,' is already expressing an opinion." As long as we relate to things indirectly, as ideas, we see through filters of hope, expectation, opinion, point of view, etc. But looking through a filter is not the same as simply seeing what's there: seeing the flower. Or looking at and seeing the person sitting across from us without an obscuring judgment. Just seeing: seeing the mountain, the river, our partners and co-workers, the earth, our children. Seeing what is, just as it is.

Mortenson describes the dilemma perfectly when he recognizes the difference between seeing K2 as a goal, and then seeing it. Period. It probably cannot be said more clearly. When we simply see what's before us, we begin to recognize that the whale moving through the water is just a different expression of a force whose truth of being is K2—and us as well. One source gives rise to life and is embedded in life. Everything that's alive is a revelation of this presence. This is why the mystics and poets insist that there is no separation, and why they write about one spirit in all creation. Johannes Metz says, "Our power and strength are derived from the wellsprings of invisible mystery." Paul of Tarsus writes, "For in him we live and move and have our being" (Acts 17:28). The seers recognize that our deepest nature is unencumbered, and that in knowing that, we are able to live increasingly unafraid. Metz goes on, "This spirit . . . is the doorway through which men must pass."

The whales are already a pure and full expression of spirit. They do not struggle; they are what they are. This is the thrill of being in their presence—they put us immediately in touch with the underglimmer. It is more complicated for human beings. Hampered by ego, we do not effortlessly know our deeper nature and do not express it with freedom. There are many false beliefs to unmask before we see more clearly. We grow up believing that we are our personalities, our occupations, our gender or race—the roles we play. We look at our bodies and say, this is me. But all of these things are either attributes of human nature or experiences we've had, but not who we most deeply are. The truth of us still lies hidden.

By deciding what really matters we take a first step toward awareness. We question what we've been clinging to and notice how we are relating to life. Am I experiencing life directly, or am I only experiencing life through my thoughts and beliefs? Do my thoughts bring me happiness and a sense of peace? Is there something else, something beyond the surface of things?

The mind cannot offer a direct experience in response to our curiosity. The only entry point is this very day.

The life I am living is not the same as the life that wants to live in me.

—Parker Palmer, *Let Your Life Speak*

2

It's Never Too Late to Start Over

A few years ago an experience I had with a group of women deeply affected me. The setting was a stone chapel in the hills north of San Diego. It was dusk, and the only light in the room came from a table filled with candles and the muted glow of several gaslit sconces. There were a handful of wooden pews, and women were filing in slowly—a classical guitarist played softly in the background. It was the last night of a five-day stay at a beautiful health and fitness spa. The next morning everyone would be returning to airports and busy schedules—all of life's ongoing challenges. I had been there offering a seminar each afternoon for anyone interested in attending. This evening was a final gathering.

I watched as the women entered the light of this picturesque setting and then settled into the silence. I knew many of their stories now and knew that appearances are deceiving. Behind some of the smiles were hidden heartaches and regrets, something true not only for the women sitting in this chapel but for many of us. The human heart holds myriad secrets.

One of the women had eaten lunch with me earlier in the day, the first time she and I had had an opportunity to speak directly. She'd been forthright; there was something on her mind. She leaned across the table and looked into my eyes to ask one question: "Is it ever too late to heal . . . to begin again?"

I searched her eyes and knew that the answer to this question held great weight for her. If healing isn't possible, if there is a limit to our ability to grow and to take new steps, then what? If there isn't a second or third chance to learn what we haven't yet understood, then life has the power and force to defeat us. She was asking, is there a point beyond which starting over is not an option? Or is there always hope?

She didn't share a single detail of her life story, but it was there in her eyes. Even without knowing the particulars, I could tell that she, like most of us, probably lived with some regret. She might feel shame about some past action. Perhaps she'd made choices that she now believes were in error. There might be spoken words she wishes she had never uttered. Or perhaps there was a path she found the courage to pursue—and then unforeseen complications developed, making it seem impossible to either move forward or to undo what was now unfolding. Had fear caused her to be less than honest with herself? Looking into her eyes I saw every possibility. And then, given the circumstances known only to her, this question: Is it too late to begin again? She wanted to know.

My mind raced as I considered many things to say in reply . . . things I probably felt would be helpful, and perhaps one or two of them would have been. But I finally answered the question by simply saying, "No, it's never too late to heal and start anew."

It is not too late because life is this moment, and only this. There is now—this day—and its full potential to open wide a new door. And even though we may tremble at the immediacy and intimacy of the thresholds we face, there is within us the power to walk through these new openings. There is within us a power greater than anything we will ever face, greater than anything we have ever done—a power that enables us to learn from our missteps and begin again.

Men and women actively involved in twelve-step programs are living testaments to the human capacity to start over. But equal courage arises in prisons, halfway houses, jails . . . and on very ordinary streets in unassuming homes in the neighborhoods where you and I live. The externals are irrelevant. The courage to begin again rises up from within. An ordinary moment is suddenly imbued with possibility, and you take a first step. You turn away from the shadows, that is, the seeming power of your circumstances, and turn toward life. In the act of turning, the power to exceed what appeared to be insurmountable is available.

Beginning again is possible because life is possible. We can choose to go on, entering into the fullness that is at the heart of all things. Starting over is the step we take because of a small vow we make to ourselves: I choose to live. I choose to heal and grow. I agree to meet the circumstances in my life with the power of spirit that lies within.

After sitting in silence for a while in the chapel that evening, I spoke a few words of encouragement to those who had gathered. Our group was a microcosm of the world, a small number of people reaching to find compassion for others and for themselves. We were learning that to step out onto a new road means letting go of a measure of control in exchange for the new freedom.

I'd left several of the candles on the front table unlit. Now I invited each woman to light a candle in honor of some cause or person, somewhere in the world, where hope was dim. The woman with whom I'd spoken at lunch was one of the last persons to come forward. The first match she struck burned out before she could summon the composure to speak. Striking a second match she managed to say, "I light this candle for anyone who needs to know that you can always begin again." I listened to her simple prayer, knowing that it applied to untold men and women who question whether or not they can actually meet life in a new way. And I thought of those who will never even ask the question, as she had—those who will live unaware of a power that is theirs. I thought of those who believe, "I will never get over this," or have convinced themselves that there is no way out. The light from her candle reached out to bless a multitude. She herself was making a turn at that very moment by walking forward and speaking her prayer out loud. Flames from all the candles lit her face. And it was, as it always is, quite magnificent to see the force of life rising up in its beauty.

Life contains a variety of sobering realities. There are relationships we'd like to repair but simply cannot, either because the other person is not willing, or has died, or has perhaps moved on in his or her own life. There are others we long to help but who will not receive our assistance for a number of reasons. Sometimes they are simply not ready. But our own healing does not depend upon (or demand) being able to turn any situation around. It is about turning *ourselves* around. It is about beginning to see what we formerly couldn't see and taking a step toward living differently. In the process we develop compassion for each soul who struggles with the human journey.

We sometimes mourn how certain things in our life unfolded. This is natural. But in the end, we cannot go back. There is only this day. This is where life takes place. The day in front of me is life.

When Rachel Naomi Remen was well into her sixties she recalled a moment in childhood when she saw two tender blades of green grass growing through a New York City sidewalk—not through a crack in the sidewalk but right through the cement. "I thought I understood a lot about power," she says in an NPR interview, "but I'd never witnessed this kind of power before."

At the time she had just been told by a team of doctors that she had a disease with no cure. She was fourteen years old, and the doctors cruelly predicted that she would be dead by forty. She remembers the physicians' words as "a death sentence with all the power of science behind it. No one said, 'It's possible that there is something in you that science can't measure . . . something that might be able to break through this obstacle and find a way to live.'"

If the doctors had known, they might have told her to bring the force of her spirit to bear on the situation she faced. They might have reminded her that she was more than the surface of things—that who we most deeply are is not limited by our circumstances. They might have told her to listen to all the questions that would arise in the ensuing years. Listen well, they might have advised her, because these are the questions you have to ask—the questions inspired by an inner depth whose sole intention is to guide you. These are the questions that will push against you and will not let you go, the questions that will not accept something simply because it is familiar or has always been thought about in a particular way. These are the questions that will save you and help you take the first step in a different direction: Is there a deeper meaning to my life, a deeper purpose for being here? Does loneliness have something to teach me? Or limitation? Where does my feeling of life's unfairness come from? What do I believe I am entitled to have or hold? And how will I see anything new with my mind so proud, crowded with the conclusions I have already drawn? Can I see past my long-held views to something broader and greater? Am I willing? Is there something more than moving through life in a trance, watching the years pass and wondering where time has gone?

Will I let life plow through my field and turn the soil until the moist, richer humus beneath the surface is uncovered? Can I watch the stones of my mistaken beliefs fly like bullets, fleeing the force of the blade that wants to clear the way? Am I able to look at myself and walk on, a refugee from my old conclusions, and let something else teach me? Do I have enough courage to put my meager belongings in a sack and head out? How much am I really willing to know, and how hard will I work to find it?

We have a deeper nature, greater than any other power. This inner nature is not a brushed-up tale from yesterday. It is a new alphabet. "Are you brave enough to awaken?" the teacher had asked me. Are you brave enough to reach toward the spirit that lies within and let it be your guide?

Several years ago a manuscript was sent to me for evaluation. In the story a woman walks through a cemetery and finds words engraved on a tombstone: *Leave the Ashes, Take the Fire.* It is a perfect description of the healing path, explained in six words, seven syllables: Let go what is past and move on. The power to change course is in us, but each person must demand this of themselves—you cannot decide for someone else. Everyone you love is on their own journey. We alone possess the means to experience life differently for ourselves. We can take the fire and create a new beginning.

In 2000 Eve Ensler inaugurated a writing group at the Bedford Correctional facility in New York state. For four years a group of female inmates sat with her as she created a place of safety strong enough for them to tell one another their stories. The circle they formed was a knot that life and drugs and single moments of passion and misjudgment had drawn tight. The knot was thorny, a tangle of threads that the years had weathered. Still, the women unraveled the knot and said the difficult words behind which were swells of humiliation and shame. Some of their acts were ruinous.

Within the circle they learned that if they were defeated in the end, it would not be because of the crimes they had committed. It would be the disappointment and sadness that grew up around those acts like weeds, choking off light and hope. In addressing the prison population Ensler reflected, "You have been *frozen* in your mistakes."

So the inmates sat together in a circle month after month and began to take responsibility for what they had done. Healing was a slim dream at first, a small piece of kindling with the task of burning away a lifetime of defeat and regret. Some mistakes had happened in a moment; some occurred over a period of time. The women now faced what they had done and confronted the heavy weight of their own self-judgment. They were heroic to watch as they began to see themselves not as unforgivable, but as human beings who had made serious mistakes. They became moles burrowing deep into the earth, hunting for the self-compassion that would be their food and light. Ensler said to them, "There is the mistake. It is one moment. It is in the past . . . It cannot be changed. Then, there is the woman."

The same clarity flows through the memorable line from the book *Kite Runner* by Khaled Hosseini. "There is a way to be good again."

In the center of life lies a hidden freedom. In this core the chaff is separated from the grain. This freedom says that we don't have to remain who we've always been or repeat old choices. The past does not have ultimate authority to dictate the future. There is a powerful self in us that is able to change our course. We can begin anew. It's not a matter of summoning the strength to pull ourselves up by the bootstraps. This is not a mental exercise. It's not a matter of *doing* anything. It's a matter of letting the misperceptions fall away until the deeper self emerges. You put aside the old way of thinking/looking and just look. Then, for a split second you realize that we all see so much less than we're able to see—that there's more. And you ask to be shown the way.

This is what Gerald May experienced when he said to the forest, "Take me in." He was waking up to the day before him. He had already made a thorough inventory of his past and openly mourned his losses. Now he was able to see the beauty and power contained in each moment. He knew that life was not the stream of thoughts produced by the mind. Life is not an idea. Life is in front of us. Poet David Whyte offers, "Leave everything you know behind and open both arms."

Writer and teacher Pema Chodron states it very practically: "Your life is your working base." You start over by learning to protect that working base. You stop telling yourself limiting things because words have power. *This will never work. I'll never get over this. I can't. I'm not good enough.* Instead, you focus your attention in a different direction. Which lesson is life bringing to me? What should I notice? Is my schedule too busy? Am I challenging myself enough? Am I burying my pain? Am I overtaxing my body? What did I pay attention to today, and is that focus fruitful? Am I creating a life that is nourishing or one that undermines me? Am I secretly clinging to something that distracts me or weighs me down? Who or what do I ask to make me happy?

There are no instant answers. Beginning again necessitates the careful sowing of new harvests. But by spending the time to develop new capacities—by learning to know ourselves in a fuller way—the seed of change begins to germinate.

Following my vision quest, I took an hour-long walk in the park every morning for ten years. It was my means of nurturing silence and developing a relationship with both Nature and myself. As I walked along I paused often, standing before a tree or a flower to simply look. My commitment to this walk did not immediately appear to be beneficial—at least, outwardly. Taking time to notice the color of the leaves, or the angle of light on the path, I had no amazing revelations, no theological thoughts. I could not see any obvious benefit from spending an hour in this way; there were no measurable markers. But in hindsight, the intrinsic value of setting aside that hour has revealed itself. Because of that commitment something new began to forge itself in me. As I walked, my eye and ear were being trained to watch for the underglimmer. Day by day I was putting my energy in a new direction. I was creating the building blocks for a different journey. The new awareness did not develop quickly. I had to put in my time.

Renowned Vietnamese monk Thich Nhat Hanh says, "Our daily practice usually consists in running away." I was now making a commitment to stay. I wanted to bring something into my daily life that would support my waking up, and I was supporting that decision with my actions. I intuitively knew that no amount of thinking or study would get me where I wanted to go. I had to show up and learn to be present to the day at hand.

Writing had taught me something about this process. When I slack off and begin to write infrequently, my writing is no longer tight and focused. Instead, it requires a lot of editing and re-writing. But if I'm working steadily on a manuscript and have been writing daily for forty or fifty days, each day's offering becomes increasingly strong and powerful.

Starting over is a matter of practice. It's a matter of developing an intimate relationship with your deepest self, and this means spending time with yourself and with all that is. The fuel that powers change is a growing intimacy with what is. There is nothing mystical about this; it simply requires desire and discipline. It's a matter of making a commitment. You decide to put energy and attention into noticing the present day.

You notice when you're lost in thought and pull yourself back to the present moment. You practice seeing the person before you as someone vitally alive and essentially unknown to you, and discipline yourself not to look at him (or her) through a familiar filter of who you think he is. Or you take a walk and pause frequently, no longer taking in trees, in general, with a sweeping glance. You look at this particular flower that is right before you—or notice the tree bowing in the wind at your window. As you cook you become increasingly present to each ingredient, mindful of textures and smells. You remember to do one thing at a time. The smell of the sage will be diminished if you are also watching television or talking on the phone as you create the meal. You embrace things simply and directly and the present moment comes alive.

Day by day you become aware of the feast life offers—a feast that is right in front of you. In the words of poet John O'Donohue, "You [begin to engage] the infinite design." He goes on, "Every life is braided by luminous moments." It is never too late to see them. You can begin again right now. You pause and look. The stopping creates the opening.

Taking a step in a different direction, I unravel the knot of past actions and old conclusions. It's never too late to begin again.

—Paula's journal

3

Align Yourself with Life: Move the Way Life Is Moving

On the road from Anchorage to Homer, Alaska, there is an unusual flow of water hidden behind tall grasses. There is nothing remarkable about the spot at first. All you see is a stream of water flowing alongside the road. But if you stand there for a while you are taken in by the effortlessness of the water's movement as it flows between the grasses and disappears around a bend. It begins to have a mesmerizing beauty. You note elegance in the way the water rushes by without pause or restriction, carrying life in its current. It gives the appearance of something that is silky and serene, pulling you toward a hidden incandescence. The setting is not perfect. On all sides of the water is life as it is: berry bushes, stalks of dead grass, the speed of traffic, the shadow of clouds passing over the grasses. Yet within this small cove of concealed loveliness an unimpeded flow of water gleams and moves without resistance from its source.

This sweet stream is a powerful teacher. Move the way life

is moving, I hear it say. Move with life, not against it. When you move against life, you're not only in opposition to the essential life force, but you're also forcing other things to adopt an unnatural pace. You end up interfering with the underlying perfection of things. Aligning with life demands our powerful acquiescence.

Slowing down to move at life's more measured pace is an access point to the day at hand. All life moves in harmony with a single power. Nature never violates this rhythm, but human beings do. Our fears and opposition to life take us further and further away from the source that sustains us.

Several years ago sixteen of us from four different countries and all walks of life were moving through a field of wheat at dusk. We were pilgrims making our way from Paris to the Cathedral at Chartres, France, an important stop on all major medieval pilgrimage routes to Santiago, Rome, and Jerusalem. My water bottle made a small slapping noise against my backpack as I walked. This was the third day, the last of our fifteen-mile days. That night we'd arrive in Chartres.

We walked stretched out in a ragged line. I was tired and would be glad for the hostel and a warm bed. But with just a few miles to go we were overtaken by a fast-moving storm. We covered up with rain gear, but within minutes water soaked our heads and slid down our necks and backs. My cotton pants became two wet rags that clung to my thighs as I pushed on, creating a cold, damp pressure on my legs. The gales of rain were chilly and intense; none of us had adequate protection. Our backpacks, sneakers, jackets—everything—were quickly soaked.

Lightning sent a powerful bolt through the sky ahead. Then another. The field lit up once, fiercely, and then it was dark. Heads bent, we trudged on. There were no alternatives, no shelter. We were soggy figures moving through wet stalks of grass like colorful tokens on a game board. The spires of the cathedral were now visible and encouraging, but each step forward seemed such a small gain.

By the time we finally reached the cathedral we were clammy and cold, drenched to the skin. Rain beat onto our faces and dripped into our eyes. I tilted back against the weight of my pack to look up at the great height of the edifice that we'd been walking toward for the last several days. The soaking rain made it difficult to see very much. I tried to shield my eyes with my arm and took a step backward. And in the next moment the downpour became irrelevant.

The cathedral was magnificent.

I stood before her shyly. Hundreds of layers of carefully placed stone towered above us, commanding respect. Something within me fell silent. For the first time I was aware of the meaning of making a pilgrimage. There have been thousands of pilgrims over the centuries, and now I was one of them. The unbearably difficult task of building this structure in the Middle Ages overwhelmed me. I sensed the effort of nameless laborers who built this structure by hand in order to elevate the human spirit. I could feel their breath as close as my own. My heart whispered *thank you*, but the words were pitiful compared to the gift.

Our guide, Gernot, signaled for us to follow, and we walked quietly behind the cathedral, our wet jackets catching the wind as it blew against the stone. Each person was deep in private thought until we reached the 150 steps that lead to the pilgrim's entrance. My legs protested, but I put one wet foot in front of the other and found the first step. Midway I stop counting, and my body found a rhythm that carried me forward.

Our only intention that evening was to see the cathedral from the outside, standing there before the pilgrim's door. We'd sleep in a nearby hostel within the cathedral's shadow and enter the next morning with the first light. But a poster announcing a procession to the Black Madonna that evening caught our eyes, and the synchronicity of arriving on this very night was too irresistible. We decided not to wait until morning. Pulling at the massive doors, we looked inside to find the procession.

We were, I imagine, like many pilgrims over the centuries— bone-weary and burdened by the affairs of our individual lives. Yet as the ancient doors opened and we stepped through, everything else dropped away.

A surprising power filled the great void. There is the impression of air soaring up to the heights above, and I felt myself lifted as well. Arriving was no longer the goal. This was it. This was the cathedral at Chartres. I crossed the threshold and let the space take me in.

That night and for the following two days I opened myself to her tremendous presence as I crawled over every inch of the great Gothic sanctuary. As a group we lit candles in the crypt, walked the ancient stone labyrinth, and watched light refracted by the mosaics of stained glass. I sat alone in the darkness of the pews listening to visiting choirs, and sat outside in the sun, my back against the stone. I remained within her walls for hours, and I had barely begun my exploration. I stared at the statue of the Black Madonna, led back to her small chapel over and over again. I found myself laying flowers there but cannot recall the mind's decision to do so. I didn't question anything; I let myself go wherever I was taken.

On the final day of our stay a guide from the cathedral took us high above the tower stairwells until we were in the space beneath the roof. From there we walked one by one down a wooden catwalk and tasted the soaring vastness of the nave and the brilliance of the labyrinth as seen from above. Through a knothole in the catwalk boards we knelt to see the rose at the center of the labyrinth, hundreds of feet below. The beauty of that single flower seen from such height is inexpressible. I felt as if I were seeing my own life from a great, great distance. Looking at the rose I knew, without hesitation, that everything it had taken for me to live my life and meet its challenges was the perfect unfolding of an invisible force that had guided me since the day I was born.

Afterward, in the last hours of sunlight, I sat on a bench in front of the cathedral and wondered how I would feel in the morning as we boarded the trains that would take us back into hectic lives and demanding schedules. I have seen few, if any, places of historical significance in this way—from the inside out. It was a great gift to have the leisurely schedule that allowed us to explore the building at a slow pace. But as I watched tour buses drop people off for an hour's visit and then whisk them away again, I knew it was the way we approached the cathedral that made the essential difference. We'd moved toward her in a manner that reflected and honored her presence. We were moving with her for all those miles.

Before leaving the United States I read about her and studied photographs. I walked several miles a day for months in preparation for the pilgrimage time. I imagined her as I walked on different streets, an ocean away, where people live and work and express their love far from the shadows of these towers. I carried her image long before I arrived in France. And though I knew I could never know her fully, I still walked lovingly through her chapels and down her long aisles, wanting to know as much of her as I could. I walked with respect for her power and beauty, for the artistry of her stained glass, and the coolness of her marble. In my mind I heard the footfalls of those who brought her into being and felt the invisible link between their brief lifetimes and my own.

I had approached her carefully, aligning myself with the rhythm of our pilgrimage and the nature of her looming presence. And it became clear that if I had moved toward her quickly and casually, distracted by the usual clamor of 10,000 things, parts of her would have remained invisible to me, even though photographs would prove that I had been there. I also realized that if I'd arrived with a mental picture of her set too firmly in my mind, I wouldn't have seen her in the same way. I would have seen that image instead.

I had to be willing to slow down and move the way life is moving. "Life in the west is up to ninety miles an hour," observed John O'Donohue, "and at ninety miles an hour you can be up to many things, but not presence." I had to join life, move with her . . . feel her lifeblood in my own. The Chartres cathedral was more than another French monument, and the pilgrimage was more than the novelty of being on the ancient pilgrim's route. I had to surrender my prior image of the Cathedral as well as my image of the others who walked beside me. I had to release those stories like kites flung into the clouds and approach the truth of the Cathedral and the reality of my fellow pilgrims instead. Sitting on the bench outside the Cathedral that afternoon, it was clear that the way you approach something (or someone) deeply affects everything that follows—it determines what you see. I saw that the heart's willingness to move *with* life, to allow circumstances and experiences to become the path, is a great variable. On this fulcrum so much turns. I could see how many experiences and people I had missed, even when standing right before them for years.

This time I had slowed down and moved the way life was moving. I approached Chartres with a measured pace. I did not enter with my own agenda. I moved into her soaring interior with a simple *yes*, which opened my heart.

Moving the way life is moving seems, at first blush, to imply giving up, or "going along with," but nothing is further from the truth. Accepting the life before us is actually an expression of vitality. It speaks of an inner alignment with spirit—an alliance that reflects the perfection of life and the underlying life force.

On the pilgrimage I noticed that the longer we walked, the more our minds cleared. We experienced what it is like to slow down and take things in. Our pace gradually created an environment free from the usual distractions; we simply experienced the day before us. We were moving in a space of aliveness.

In accepting life as it is I begin to look at things directly. Some circumstances require action. Yet there is a great distinction between reactions prompted by the ego and action that arises from a deep awareness of life's flow. The former is reactive and controlling, and serves self-interest. The latter is forceful and clear. Action that arises from a profound acceptance of life is always in the service of love.

The Native American sweat lodge provides another way of thinking about moving the way life is moving. The lodge is one of the most recognized of all Native American ceremonies and is a traditional way of facilitating healing and purifying body, mind, and spirit. The lodge itself is a domed hut built from willow saplings or some other supple wood. Stones are heated in an exterior fire and then brought into the covered lodge and placed in a central pit that's been dug into the ground. When water is poured on the stones it creates dense steam.

During my first lodge I was fearful of the reported heat that rises up from those stones. I knew that some persons have to leave the lodge because the intensity of heat is so great. Yet when we received our final instructions from the lodge keeper his advice to us was, "Don't resist the heat." He told us that resistance would cause our experience of the heat to worsen. Instead, he encouraged us to let go of our resistance and befriend the heat. "Welcome the heat by acknowledging its presence," he said, "and your experience will transform."

At the time, his words were a marked departure from the way I'd always thought about things. "Don't resist," he advised. "Acknowledge what is." I'd always believed that by resisting the things I wanted to change, I would exert the greatest power. Now I was learning otherwise. Only by first acknowledging and accepting what is—including the things I cannot change, or do not want or expect to happen—do I possess the true strength to meet life. Life calls us to meet it as it is. In acknowledging what is, respect for life is implicit. When acceptance precedes doing, then the steps we take have a distinct clarity and power.

The same dynamic applies to acceptance of ourselves. Zen teacher Joko Beck reflects, "In times of confusion and depression the worst thing we can do is to try to be some other way. [When] we experience ourselves as we are, not the way we think we should be . . . a gate opens."

I once turned on the television in a hotel room to get a weather report while traveling. A fanciful movie was just ending. It was about "human" mermaids who lived both on land and sea. In the story, one of the mermaids was about to return home to the sea for the last time. The camera angle was wide. The mermaid entered the water from the shore and began moving slowly into deeper water. The ocean filled the screen. Waves covered more and more of the mermaid's advancing body until I had the sensation of being pulled by the same tide myself. Water continued to rise up until the mermaid's head disappeared completely and there was only sea. Long after the movie credits rolled I was still standing in the corner of the hotel room feeling the strength of that image.

It might be said that our own lives are always moving either toward the sea (our deeper nature) or away from it. The effect of our moving away from life's intrinsic design is that we end up living in opposition to who we most deeply are. Joko Beck comments, "We humans, with probably the most immense gifts of any creature, are the only beings on earth that say, I don't know the meaning of my life. I don't know what I'm here for. No other creature is confused like that." Purpose and fullness can only be found when we align with life and learn to accept what is. I may not be able to change my circumstances, but in accepting what is I align myself with the way life is moving.

During my own period of grief, moving with life meant not resisting the sadness. It was there. The loss had happened. I had to acknowledge what could not be changed. In accepting what was, I opened up to the life before me and created the space in which healing could begin. I learned that the way I live *this* moment, right now, is the way I am living my life, and if I am not awake to this day, then I am missing life's potential and depriving myself of its healing power. I may stubbornly insist that life be different than it is, but my insistence does not change anything. Healing is only available in this moment.

What is, is. In aligning with the life before us, we begin to flow like that hidden stream as it moves from its source—the same way the mermaid yielded to the tide.

Thomas Merton reflects, "When we are strong we are always much greater than the things that happen to us, and the soul of a man who has found himself is like a deep sea in which there may be many fish: But they never come up out of the sea, and not one of them is big enough to trouble its placid surface. His 'being' is far greater than anything he feels or does."

Everything on earth is being continuously transformed, because the earth is alive . . . and it has a soul. We are part of that soul.

—Paulo Coelho, *The Alchemist*

4

Give Up Expecting Life to Be a Certain Way

The summer when I was sixteen years old I spent an unforgettable six weeks in Europe as an exchange student studying German at one the universities in Austria. As summer ended I prepared to cross the English Channel with a small group of fellow students. We were all returning to the United States, many of us reluctant to have our experiences abroad end.

Hearts and emotions were high. A boat trip across a famous sea, then London to explore before heading home. We'd heard about this channel crossing and seen it in news clips and movies. We ran up the gang plank and edged and shoved to get the perfect spot at the rail. A whoop went up when we left the dock. We stood and watched the shoreline of France recede. Minute by minute houses and monuments were swallowed back into the skyline. A whole continent disappeared, blended back into sea and sky, the horizon moving like a skilled painter who decided to erase the lower part of the canvas.

But very quickly our romantic notions about fading cities and crossing the channel came to an end. We had barely been at sea when the boat pitched for the first time, sending everything that was not securely tied down flying across the deck. Someone shouted. Everything was banging and knocking about. The boat pitched again, and we were riding up and down the backs of waves that were now great, blue-grey swells. We continued to rise up and fall back down with everyone hanging on to whatever was available. Many were sick but could do nothing about it. We were at the mercy of uncommonly high, rough waters, and however long it actually took to make that crossing, it felt twice as long. English soil, solid British earth underneath our feet was inexpressibly dear when it came. I practiced taking a step or two, but the trick of the mind still told me that I was in motion. We held on to one another and staggered along until we'd all re-adjusted to the security of steady ground.

My anticipation of the channel crossing—the image I had in my mind prior to the actual trip—bore no resemblance to the voyage we'd actually experienced, and once we were re-established on solid earth, I was aware of feeling cheated. It wasn't supposed to be a harrowing crossing; it was supposed to be breathtaking. It was supposed to be the crowning end to our summer adventure.

The crossing—complete with strong wind and high seas—differed greatly from the way I'd thought and hoped our voyage would be. In one hand were my dreams and expectations; in the other the reality of a rough time at sea. That very dilemma—the gulf between your expectation of life, and life itself—would become a theme central to my life's journey. Being young, I didn't guess the power of expectation, nor did I see the challenge and importance of learning to receive life as given.

In the months following the death of my family, my resistance to life as it is was never more pronounced. The stark reality I faced was far removed from the dream I'd held for my life. Sadness and envy pulled at my skirts, refusing to let me make peace with these circumstances I hadn't chosen and didn't want.

My eyes were lasers, keen hunters that found the homes where whole families lived—the ones with mothers, fathers, and siblings—families that lived the way I thought life should be. I kicked at the reality of my own circumstances with my toe and watched puffs of entitlement rise up in response. I didn't want the life being held out to me. That was the truth I was not speaking out loud. My secret thought was that there were two lives: the one I was supposed to have, and the crummy one I'd gotten.

Questions arose in that dark: Can you find love even in these circumstances? Can you see beauty in exactly what you've been given? Can you receive life as offered, even though it isn't what you had in mind? Can you live on life's terms, and not your own?

The questions were deeply demanding and I resented them. They were arrows aimed at my sense of entitlement. The truth was that I felt sorry for myself, as well as deprived, and just for good measure, very justified in feeling this way. Could I (would I) receive life as given? I didn't know. The questions nailed me to the wall my life had become, the wall on which I was pounding out my grief and pain. Would I let go of the first script, the one I was insisting upon, including the idea that I deserved specific things? Would I move past my sense that there was a way things should be? My first response was no, I would not.

The first script said that pain was the enemy. Even though this conclusion brought me no peace, I continued to see life and pain as my adversaries. I was convinced that there was a better way—my life should have unfolded differently. In addition, I felt singled out for suffering, a view that validated my righteousness and my growing hardness of heart. I fully believed that my troubles were all the result of my circumstances. Since the life I was living seemed to justify these feelings, my rising anger went unexamined, and the rest of the needy world became invisible to me. There I was, left alone with my unexamined, life-leaching first script—one I was apparently willing to risk everything defending.

One afternoon, my heart breaking, I began sorting through the clothes my daughter Sarah would never wear. A dress lay across my lap, a little piece of white cotton. It evoked one more moment (there were many) of bitter tears and confused disbelief. This was not the life I had chosen. It was not the life I expected. Life was not supposed to turn out this way.

My fingers lingered on the weave of the cloth and the soft starch in the fabric. It was such an innocent and common thing—a child's garment. Yet even as it broke my heart, that dress became an opening; the soft cotton tore at me from within and began to empty me.

You are not the only heartbroken parent in the world, it said. The pain of loss is not yours alone. Disappointment is the human condition. I continued to stare at cotton and lace, but something had shifted. The dress was somehow connecting me to the texture and mystery of greater things, and it began to shed a faint, life-changing light. It was untying me from my moorings. As I looked at the fabric I saw what I'd previously been unable to see: that there were many mistaken beliefs to which I was deeply tethered, and I could not move forward until I decided to let them go. I had to meet life as it is, not as I imagined it or wanted it to be.

Richard Rohr writes, "Life becomes problem-solving, fixing, explaining, and taking sides with winners and losers. It can be a pretty circular . . . existence. We have to allow ourselves to be drawn into sacred space, often called liminality. All transformation takes place there. The old world is left behind, but we're not sure of the new one yet . . . In sacred space the old world is able to fall apart, and the new world is able to be revealed."

Without fully understanding why, I began to soften. I saw life's contour, its density and its brilliance, just as it is, nothing more. I saw the way I'd sought security in things that are impermanent, and how I had insisted on them. I saw the meaning I'd assigned to things that are fleeting, just like this dress. I saw how I'd been caught in a script of my own creation and was having a tantrum like a two-year-old now that it wasn't going my way. How self-centered I'd become—or maybe always was, but now I knew. I was totally caught up in my own world—my emotions, my wants, and my needs. There was a greater world beyond my borders but I'd been oblivious to it. The truth was that I was hardly alone with my broken heart. And comparatively, I had lived like the elite. Now it was simply my time—my turn to know the darkness and discover whether or not I was brave enough to accept the human journey and find a way through. Holding the dress, I stepped outside of my own script for the first time and considered that human life has a greater purpose. Perhaps the dress, my daughter, and all that had been might lead me to that knowledge if I was willing to let go of my demands that life be a certain way. I needed to release my grip and just look. "All great spirituality," writes Rohr, "is about letting go."

I slowly began to see that within the cells of every living thing is the same essence—the presence of spirit. The heart of our journey is to awaken to this spirit within. The point is not to have a perfect life and realize every expectation. Something else is at work in life—something with a totally different purpose. I'd spent enough years devoted to how I wanted (expected) life to be. Now it was time to turn to life as it is and begin that pilgrimage.

A prison inmate once looked me squarely in the eyes and confessed that she had sold drugs to purchase coffins for her two young sons who were killed in a fire. We sat there together in the stark room set aside for counseling. There was not a bit of beauty in that décor. No picture, no lovely fabric, no color. I didn't move as she described her life—a life far removed from the way she thought life should be. Her actual life was in opposition to all the images she dreamed when she was an innocent girl of six or seven. She didn't get a beautiful, desirable childhood. Instead she got poverty and heartache. As an adult she suffered through the unthinkable grief of losing two children while in prison, an atmosphere where it wasn't safe to cry or show any vulnerability. All her screams were silent.

Then she began to write poetry in a small journal. Word by brave word her heart raged. Anger and pain roared through her pen, striking out with venom. They heaved and bucked through her until she began to write something else. She found a first shred of gratitude for some small favor. Then another. She remembered a kind gesture and a genuine smile—one sincere connection. The gratitude softened her. She knew full well that there were women in that prison who were bent double with life's injustices and their own versions of pain. So she reached out to someone, and then another someone, and another . . . until she came to terms with the life that was hers.

She found a way to sit down with the life before her and let it begin to speak. She wondered out loud, in front of me, if some of her suffering might have been generated because she was holding on too tightly to the way she thought things should be? She didn't look up for an answer. Didn't need to. She'd spoken the words to get them out there, threw them into the ring like a knife thrown by an expert arm. She smiled faintly and kept reading.

The last time I saw her she was sitting astride a big tractor, mowing the lawn in the prison courtyard. She was wearing headphones and singing away to music, swaying in response to the beat. I waved a hand and she rode over to where I was standing and cut the engine. There was a big grin on her face. "Today is my last day here." Bigger grin. We high fived one another. "Last day!"

Amazing how much there was to say and yet no words to hold it. There we stood, sun streaming down indiscriminately on the barbed wire surrounding the prison yard as well as the free side of the wall. The guards were restless. I was leading a retreat in a different cell block and needed to get on my way. The guards wanted me to move.

Nothing's reasonable, I thought. Hardly anything turns out the way you expected it to, and you're frequently ready to write life off as too paradoxical and too difficult to endure. Then some indescribable light fights its way through the impenetrable dark—an unpredictable, unimportant, runaway moment that lights up everything you've been unable to see until then. That light removes all the shoulds and oughts, all the illusions about fairness. You enter liminal space, that time, says Rohr, "where nothing looks like what [you're] used to—the realm where God can best get at us because we are out of the way." In that space you take your first script, the one that weighs five hundred pounds, the script that was cutting into your heart all along, bleeding you to death but you didn't realize the wound or its seriousness—and you simply let it go.

"Listen," I said to the inmate, "have a great life." She was already putting her protective goggles back on. She gave me a thumbs up, laughed out loud, laughed right up to the sun and the clouds and the blue sky. She restarted the motor and expertly maneuvered the big engine around the edges of the flower bed, making sure the new blooms were protected.

"You too," she shouted. "You too!"

We live with expectations. Marriage is not what anyone expects; those in religious life report being surprised by the actual journey; growing up and being on your own is never what anyone expects, especially when the responsibility of earning a living settles in; raising children is never like the first picture we create in our minds. And none of this would matter, except that our expectation of things—especially the expectation we have of the people in our lives—prevents us from seeing who and what is really before us. Expectation makes us blind, and the gift of meeting the actual person who sits across the breakfast table is lost. Instead we are left with our image of that person—we are left with the mind's projection.

When couples attend a retreat together I sometimes invite them to separate and sit apart so they can watch one another from a distance. The exercise is always surprising for them. Looking across a room at someone you think you know very well creates an unusual context. You begin to realize that there are many things about this person that you really don't know. He or she is not your image of them, but very much alive. It's illuminating to watch a person well known to us—a partner, child, parent, sibling, co-worker—as if he or she were really a stranger. Subtle insights arise. By dropping our projections and images of someone else, we're free to just look. Life meets us in that moment with all its power. Everything else is a story we have made up.

The movie *Paradise Road* documents the true story of a group of women held prisoner by the Japanese during World War II. They are forced to live in inhuman conditions and endure ongoing abuse at the hands of their Japanese captors. Yet the women's capacity to endure is extraordinary, and they eventually unite, in spite of the danger, to form a vocal orchestra. With voices alone they become a symphony, and that which is most deeply embedded in life rises up within their courage. It is, as it always is, an irresistible force. Even the Japanese captors are unable to lift a hand against them—the music they create with their voices is a pure expression of spirit. In a stinking hellhole in captivity the women let go of their former, privileged lives. They see through the false illusions that have covered them like a second skin and find their way beyond them. In the very life conditions they did not expect or want they find their way to the present day. There they are suddenly, beautifully alive. Using the words of Richard Rohr, they "let go the small 'I' so that the true 'I' can be born . . . The result is, quite simply, love."

There is no way life is supposed to be. There is only life.

Fear is a no to what is.
—David Richo,
The Five Things We Cannot Change . . .

5

Make Peace with Change

A Native American friend with whom I co-led a retreat several years ago told us about his tribe's belief that during every life transition you are being renamed. He said that your name is important right from birth because it signifies something for you to become. Once named, an infant in a traditional community might be passed among two hundred arms, one to another, with each person whispering the child's name so that he or she will not forget who they are. In future years whenever that person experiences growth, a new name is given to reflect the new learning and acknowledge the new direction of his or her life.

Since the retreat was about new beginnings, the group members decided to mark their individual life changes by giving themselves a new name. At the end of the day the names were quietly recited: One who is now unafraid. She who finally dares to move forward. One who no longer lives in the past. She who knows her strength. One who accepts life with gratitude. Each man and woman spoke their new name with care, aware that making peace with change is at the core of every journey.

The reality of change is a primary human struggle. We live like people in the path of a hurricane or fire who refuse to evacuate, clinging to our familiar, well-worn versions of things and resisting what's new. As a result, important life passages become costly to navigate, which is the very reason we want to avoid them. But in avoiding the passage, we avoid the growth and the deepening as well.

If I'm honest with myself, I see that I might never have listened to life as readily years ago if the steel hand of grief and loss had not been at my back. That hand pressed me to move toward greater understanding and to suffer many changes. I didn't welcome the change. I wanted relief, not newness. Without the incentive of pain I would probably have chosen to live comfortably and securely, insisting that things stay the same. I would have innocently believed that I was in control of the things I cherished.

The ego resists change. It's that simple. It howls in protest. But the fact remains that the steel hand of grief did press against me, and in time I learned some powerful, renewable lessons: make peace with change; life must ultimately be accepted on its own terms; nothing stays the same because of our inflated wishes; life is change.

Steven Foster writes that "the first dragon you must face is the universal law of change . . . What was light must become dark, even as day becomes night. What was clear must become confusing; what was full must become empty; and what was high must be brought low. If [your] vision is to succeed, it must be tried." In accepting that fundamental characteristic of life, a pristine depth begins to emerge. A new door opens.

In 2005 I found myself unexpectedly moving from the West Coast where I had lived for two years, back to the Southwest. During a four-month period of transition while I was tying up loose ends in California and still searching for a new home in the Southwest, I rented a small, one-room apartment across the bay from San Francisco. Most of my belongings were stored with my moving company, and I was down to bare necessities. A faded beach chair was my single place to sit. A box that once held computer paper became a makeshift desk/table top. The room had a sink and a two-burner stove, but no countertop. I bought a trivet that spelled HOT in big metal letters and kept it on the floor to hold my one pot. On the broad windowsills I placed pictures of my two daughters and a pitcher that had belonged to my grandmother. My bed was a sleeping bag that I stretched out on the thin carpet. I tucked an old blanket beneath it, letting the wool supply a soft padding. Outside the window a fiery ginkgo tree was in the throes of her own change. Luminous burnt orange and yellow leaves burst from her branches that fall.

During that stretch of time everything that maintained my life was in transition, and the little rented alcove became the space in which I worked out the details. It was spare, and yet, strangely, enough. It was the space I occupied while everything shifted, the cocoon where something new began tapping steadily at my heart. For a time all I could do was learn to accept things as they were, water the flowers I kept in a vase by the window, and wait.

My initial resistance to these changes created a wall between myself and the life before me. Eventually I moved from resistance to resignation. Resignation was a small improvement, but it was still a barrier because it caused me to sink into my own gloom. I was still turning away from life, still lost in the shadows. But acceptance, when I found it, was vibrant. That was the difference. It connected me to the life force and left me in vital relationship with everything around me. This was the necessary opening that allowed something new to make itself known: I had to stand before life just as it is with a sincere compliance.

Things are as they are. I cannot change the unchangeable, but I can affect how I will respond. In choosing to meet life as it is, the journey becomes conscious of itself, and awareness grows.

During the time I spent in that small room I saw, as I had in the past, the things I was clinging to. I did a lot of soul searching and reminded myself that my points of view were just that—points of view, and not truth. Making peace with the inevitability of change became my mantra.

I noticed the tenacity of my conditioning. I watched fear move through the ether in long waves, beckoning me. What if things change, fear was quick to say. Maybe you won't be safe. But things do change. Everything passes through. Views and opinions rush downstream with the current. Health, relationships, finances—everything goes through its own cycle of transformation. Life unfolds.

In time another voice appeared—this voice was not bound by the small story of my life, nor was it driven by fear. The new voice reminded me that everything is more than it appears to be, and it asked me to consider that the hand on the blade of change is really love. It advised me that you have to awaken *within* the small story of your life in order to go beyond it. Love is a continual summons. These moments, right here, right now, are our true journey. Life is this day.

I thought of the flowers my friend Aurelia grew when she dug up her front lawn years ago. She did not plant orderly flower beds that please the mind. She planted bouquets of flowers that towered over the sidewalk and sprang up like a meadow in the city. There was an order in that garden that could not be seen until you gave up your former images of artful design. You had to realign yourself with a fresh, unfolding wholeness, a spaciousness in which it's apparent that there is an order and a beauty beyond our conventional sense of symmetry and form.

Life is change, Paula, the life force whispered. That's what life is. Life is an expression of the Divine in its many appearances and boundless disguises. Don't cling to the individual form of things; none of them last. Turn instead to the Source that brings these forms into momentary being.

When I finally moved away from that small room it was with great fondness for the time I'd spent there. The space had become a great teacher, although in very ordinary ways. The landlord had an unusual kindness about her. She would greet me as I went to and fro, looking up from her patient raking of leaves on the front lawn. She said she loved knowing that a writer was in her rooms. I later learned that she had refused to rent the room adjoining mine to a new tenant because she felt that sounds from that apartment might possibly interrupt my work. She felt that I needed the quiet. That enormous gesture was even more remarkable because the potential rent she turned aside was not insignificant to her.

In late December I handed over the keys to that wonderful space and began driving east. On New Year's Eve I stayed in an inn that was located in a small town in Arizona. It was bitterly cold. The next morning at breakfast the elderly owner of that bed-and-breakfast sat down to speak with me. He'd already exhibited a gracious spirit by opening up the inn for me when it was technically closed for the holiday. Now he was about to give me his recommendation for the morning. He had been searching my weary eyes.

"Do you mind if I speak with you frankly?" he asked. I shook my head to indicate that I would listen. "Well," he went on, "I see unhappiness in your eyes. I think you've gotten out of touch with yourself. You're too far from home," he said, pointing at his chest.

I marveled at his sensitivity and could only nod my head in response. "I want you to go to the blinking yellow light down the road," he went on, "and then turn left. In thirty minutes you'll be at the rim of the Grand Canyon. Have you ever seen it?" he asked.

I said that I hadn't. "You need to." he repeated. "Just stand there until you figure things out."

He added that no matter how hurried I felt, or how great the urgency to arrive at my destination, it was less important than going to the blinking yellow light and following the signs to the park. He was quite certain about that. I took his advice because of his extreme kindness and because I instinctively knew that he was probably right.

And he was. Something inexpressible reached through to me as I watched the sun rise over the Grand Canyon that morning. Soft waves of light glistened above those miles of furrowed rock. I watched for a long while, wrapped in a blanket, letting Earth and sun seep into my bones. I let streaming light flush the sadness away. By the time I returned to the car I had my bearings.

Life changes. That's what life does. Resisting change had only set me in opposition to life and made me feel depressed. Now I put away my trip itinerary and reached for a map in order to chart a new course. By lunchtime I was in Sedona enjoying a New Year's lunch on a small balcony. In a realistic, physical sense I was by myself, but in another sense I was not alone. I ate that meal with the landlord and the innkeeper, and the infinite expressions of life that surrounded me. The difference was that now I could see them.

The forms of things are always changing. Trees wither and drop their needles and die, people move in and out of our lives, fire and flood destroy property. Yet within each event, within every season, within the relationships that change and prove themselves to be impermanent, within the birthing and dying, and after a million things take form and then drop away—still, that which brings life into being, the unchangeable presence called God, is there. But I couldn't see that until I accepted life as change. As long as I held on tightly to my opposing view the greater knowledge was obscured.

The unchanging spirit is like a flower rising up from the secrecy of a small seed. One spirit, one heart. But only those who make peace with change will glimpse it. The rest of us are busy fighting to secure things that cannot be secured. We miss knowing that beneath the surface is our deeper nature. Beneath the surface is a greater you.

As I write, a woman of Palestinian origin who attended one of my retreats has just shipped me a package. The Middle East is embroiled in particularly violent upheavals right now, and the note she taped to her gift explains that something we spoke about during our retreat time has made an impression on her. She heard me read about Greg Mortenson's journey in Pakistan from his book, *Three Cups of Tea*. I told how three cups of tea were offered when a stranger entered a village. By the time the third cup of tea was poured, the host and guest were family. She says that the significance of drinking tea together was part of her earliest understanding.

She goes on that she has just been speaking on the phone with her father, who lives in Gaza. She mentions that he has always longed to help family members understand why misunderstandings occur and how, if left unchecked, they provoke disastrous consequences. "Maybe humankind is still pretty adolescent," she offers. "We haven't yet grown up." She reminds me that I asked her retreat group to consider the question, "What wants to be born in you?"

I finish reading her note and carefully open the wrapped package. Inside is a glass and gold tea set. It is lovelier, more delicate than can be described. It is stunning. Miraculously, nothing has broken in transit. I lift out the saucers and glasses and set them on my dining room table. It is dazzling under the light because the artistry is flawless. But it is the meaning of the tea set, and drinking tea, and humankind's great longing to exceed our warring ways that is its true brilliance. Everything I might write or could think about writing is held by those six cups.

Life is change. It is sometimes violent, often paradoxical. At some point in time this exceptional tea set will be broken, its crystal and gold buried beneath the earth to be found in a different century by a budding archeologist. Our fleeting lives are heartbreaking and also heart stopping in their beauty. And as much as we will ever know of life, even reaching to the greatest heights of our knowledge—still, it is incomparably more. The divine seed that inspires life is embedded in every cell. The mystery is beyond what the human mind can comprehend.

The timing of her gift, the gesture of it, is extraordinary. We squander so much time while a greater immensity beckons. We have to awaken within the story that is our life, and then go beyond it, in order to see. We have to wake up to this day.

Accepting change means learning about surrender and trust. It is not so much trusting that our circumstances will improve, but trusting that whatever happens, we'll find our way.

Many years ago I moved from New England to the Southwest. I left my profession as a therapist, which was my source of income. At that time I had already begun to speak, but only intermittently. I had no idea, and surely no guarantee, that I would be able to speak frequently enough to earn my living that way. The move was in response to an inner voice. I sensed that this change and relocation was right for me, but I couldn't know for sure. If I was going to do it, I had to move first, and then see.

My decision to go seemed foolhardy to more than one friend. For myself, I decided to have the experience, just once in my life, of trusting guidance from within. My practical mind bucked and rebelled to be sure, and the actual, physical move was difficult—both in leaving Boston and arriving in the new town where I'd chosen to live. If I wanted to second-guess myself, I had great cause.

But this time I surrendered to change and the unknown. I made peace with it. And that peace created a buffer of calm—something very different from the turmoil I'd experienced when making large decisions before. I learned that in the absence of my own internal opposition, which was my usual stance, life was able to meet me and help me find my way. Making peace with change was not just about accepting the inevitability that things move and fluctuate. It was about the trust and willingness to be a full participant in the life I'd been given. In the end I found so much more than a new way to earn a living. I'd stumbled upon a new way to respond to life.

To let go of having things remain the same,
to be open to change, to accept the varieties
of human predicaments . . . is rebirth into
a spiritual world.
  —David Richo,
    The Five Things We Cannot Change . . .

We awaken one day to find that the sacred
center is here and now—in every moment
of the journey, everywhere in the world
around us, and deep within our own
hearts.
  —Parker Palmer, *Let Your Life Speak*

6

Live with an Open Heart: Practice Love

One night I was trudging through hip-deep snow, trying to make my way to a small cabin in the New Hampshire woods. The snow was falling at the rate of an inch an hour, and I was fearful about lasting in the cold until I could get to a safe, warm place. Suddenly, with no obvious reason why, my inner dialogue moved from anxious, fearful thoughts into a direct experience of the snow. Something within the storm stopped me right where I was and commanded me to look. The silence I experienced dominated everything. It was open, wide. I knew without being told that this profound stillness generates life. It was also clear, in the same split-second, that this stillness is only (solely) love, and the difference between this force and any ordinary experience of love was inexpressible. For those moments, everything else vanished—my experience of the cold, my worries, any fear.

᳁

Immaculee Ilibagiza was twenty-four years old when genocide tore through her native Rwanda and she had her own direct experience of the love embedded in life. As the killing raged around her, she was taken in by a minister who hid her and seven other women in a three-by-four-foot bathroom for ninety-one harrowing days. Unable to speak to each another because of the risk of being discovered, the women were left to their inner worlds. For Immaculee this became a prolonged time of intense contemplation and prayer. She admits, "My own anger was blocking me. I felt so much fear. People were coming to kill me."

Immaculee used the long hours to listen to her innermost self and heard this advice: "If you let go anger and have love in your heart you can be okay." She took the words to heart. As the war continued to rage, an inner change had already begun. She emerged from the experience with a message of love and forgiveness for the world. Ten years later she spoke at a conference in San Antonio, Texas, and told the audience, "We have a huge world inside. We have so much power . . . Stop blaming and do your part. Our challenge is to respond differently."

Even in the face of unspeakable horror, Immaculee experienced a profound shift in her way of being. The fundamental change that took place in her was mirrored by the nature of her final response to the horrors in her country. In the heart of genocide, love called her forth. The outward event was unable to extinguish the hidden sacredness of life she had come to know. No bomb or machete could disturb the higher order of things. A life fully open to love is unassailable.

A group of us once sat in a circle for our last gathering during a weekend retreat. A woman mentioned a dream she'd had a few nights before in which she stood on a beach and watched whales just offshore. The retreat facilitator listened to her with complete attention. He suggested that she go back into her dream and see the whales again. "Describe them," he said.

Her words about the color of the water and the elegance of their leaping into the sunlight brought everyone in the room onto the beach with her. We felt the spray of grey sea and the thrill of the whales' presence. "Now shift," said the leader. "Be the whale, and look back at yourself."

As soon as her personal description of this shift had been given, we each had an opportunity to pull out our journals and write. I decided to repeat the exercise I had just witnessed and use it as the basis for my writing. In my imagination I stood on a shoreline, a woman alone, and imagined whales in the water in front of me, body to body, just as they'd been described. I imagined them towering over everything, great tons of glimmering force. In one movement they emerged from the sea, water rising up around them, white spray moving through sunlight. In my mind's eye I watched their movement as they rose from the sea and then moved back into its shadow. Then I shifted.

Now I imagined that I was the whale looking at the woman on the beach, who was me. From the vantage point of the whale, from that consciousness, I was aware of being able to express myself as any form; in that moment I had simply chosen to be a whale. I was life looking at life—consciousness looking back at a solitary figure on the beach. I could see that the woman was bound by her mental conditioning—by thought. I saw the ideas that limited her. I saw her fear and the great hold of the mind. And I wanted to free her.

I wanted her to know that as long as she believed she was only her physical body, and she remained primarily identified with her feelings and thoughts, a great restriction would define her. In essence she was something beyond that form, and her experience of separateness was an illusion. I wanted to shout this knowledge to her. As the whale I saw all of this so clearly, and I didn't want the woman to live and die without knowing it as well. If she failed to reach this awareness, I saw her predictable future.

I saw the choices she would never examine or even believe that she had, as well as the mind patterns that would prevail unquestioned. I saw how she would relate to the earth, to other humans, to adversity. I saw her years of thinking, her many assumptions, her living at the mercy of certain paradigms. I saw her accept all of this without question, believing that the continuous streams of thought going through her head were life.

How to reach her? She stood there on the beach, her bare toes curling into the sand. She loved the sunlight and the goodness of the day. As she watched, I wanted her to know the power that was hers. There was no way to measure the depth of my longing to reach her. I wanted to call across the water, "Please, let beliefs go, let go of the limiting voices. You can exceed them. Who you truly are is watching you even now. Step aside and look. Something from within you is calling."

It was an exercise, and yet not an exercise. Something had actually risen up as I wrote. A deeper me was looking back at the human form I know as myself, and that presence was aware of the story I experience as my life. Looking at myself from the eye of the whale I saw that no circumstance stood in the way of my realizing a greater freedom. *There is a spirit within not yet recognized,* was the knowledge the whale wordlessly imparted. *Beneath the surface is a greater you. We all have a chance to be here differently.*

The power to relate to life in a different way is not an attribute of our personalities or our accomplishments; it exists in our being. A true power is there. Whatever I face, I possess the means to transform my circumstances. Spirit is an indescribable force of love.

This love asks many things of us. At the time of my losses it asked me to live for a long time with very few answers and with great mystery. It asked me to find hope even in the absence of innocence. It asked me to believe that a stronger love would emerge in me . . . stronger and deeper, not in spite of my losses but because of them. Stronger, because love deepens as it passes through pain.

Love asked me to rebuild my life. It asked me to learn that letting go is not forgetting. Relationships don't end at death—they shift. They enter the heart and use a new language. Love asked me to give up my insistence on the old language and the old way of knowing in order to embrace a larger knowledge.

Love asked me to believe that healing was possible. It told me to move toward the wound until it spilled its wisdom, and then move on. "Healing," says Molly Fumia, "is a well within us that we alone can tap."

Love challenged me to grow up. If all I held onto was the pain, I'd miss the power of the love I'd also known. Was this really what I wanted? Did I want a diminished life to be the end result of having loved these two people? Love told me to fight. Fight. It's worth it. Fight to heal. Fight to recognize everything as gift. Fight to eliminate the thoughts that poison your system: unforgiveness, bitterness, regret, anger, guilt.

Love challenged me to make a list of the things that mattered in life and decide which of them were within my power. It asked me to stop focusing on what I didn't get and to focus instead on who I might become—how I might love more deeply. Love suggested that it was up to me whether or not to let life teach me, or sorrow change me. Only I could decide what to do with pain. Love said that a real power lay within, and I alone could decide whether or not to respond to its presence. Love encouraged me to take the first step forward.

When my daughter Sarah was alive I experienced my love for her only as the love between mother and daughter, and the intense bond a mother feels for her child. When that life shattered and she was gone, the pain of losing her exposed a pattern. I saw that I was living a painfully small life. The grief pushed open a door and through that doorway the power of spirit expressed itself. I saw that even though Sarah was gone, love remained. I glimpsed a purpose much greater than my individual story, and a love greater than our mother-daughter bond. I'd assigned such meaning to that love, but now a greater love beckoned.

Love waits to opens us. It shatters anything false so we can get to larger places and demands that we soften the tension between the way we want things to be and the way things are. It doesn't matter what name we give to the inner nature that drives this love, it only matters that we respond. Gerald May observed, "We don't have endless time."

A woman I met almost thirty years ago died recently. We attended the same yearly retreat for about twenty years, and she turned my heart around long ago when she approached me at the end of a retreat and told me that I was one of only two people who had ever shown her love. When she spoke those words I was painfully aware that until that moment I hadn't even really looked at her with care, let alone noticed the pain in her eyes. Although I'd apparently been kind, I hadn't seen her apart from the general retreat community—she was on the periphery of my awareness. Her words shot me through the eyes. It was terrible to realize that I was capable of living with such inattention. With that one sentence she taught me to be careful and to take time with things, with people. A real friendship grew between us. Even today, I consider her to have been one of my significant teachers. Don't turn away from what is right in front of you, her life said. Show up. Be fully present. Live into what love means.

We each struggle to understand love and to love well—to allow those whom we love to grow to their fullest potential, even to follow paths we didn't have in mind. To love is to stand before another, just as they are, and meet them with great care, not letting our own wants and needs dominate. The ego wants to fix other people and control the flow of things. It wants to be gratified.

But everyone we love is on their own journey, and we are only responsible for our own becoming. Love comes to move us past our small, distracting wants and wishes toward life itself. Even when specific circumstances dictate that we must leave or move away from a given situation, even then, we learn to move in love. We cannot embrace the full meaning of love and live the same way we were living before. The hallmark of love is the change that arises.

It is a question of what our lives generate. Am I generating a heart of dissent? A heart of judgment? A heart of complaint? A heart of love? Does my way of encountering the world serve me, or life? Do I have what it takes to grant life to others? Am I willing to cultivate a greater heart? Instead of focusing on how someone else annoys me or gratifies me—how they make me feel—can I ask the question, "What does this soul need?" The question opens a new vein.

Natalie Goldberg tells aspiring writers that "writing should be dangerous." Her description of good writing is a description of life at full throttle: daring and inviting—wholly different from our familiar patterns of politeness and safety. To live dangerously means to be intimate—to risk connecting with others. It means to be vulnerable. To move with, and to move toward. To boldly love. To ask often, what does this soul standing before me need?

Alaskan artist Brad Hughes created a work about peace in which he paints his vision of the goddess of compassion. Her look of love is the essence of the piece, as well as the most difficult aspect of the painting to put into words. You sense in her face a flush of both vulnerability and power—each arising within her deep and powerful connection to life. Still, this goddess is neither weak nor fragile. Her beauty is defined by a dazzling incandescence, her eyes a reflection of the human journey. She holds the momentary rise and fall of fortune, the seduction of cleverness and knowledge, all our secret sorrows, the moments when we question whether or not we can go on, the difficult choices upon which so much appears to rest—every worry and fear that besets humankind.

Yet present within the dilemma is the glow of her unbearable love. Her presence holds the mystery of being here in intimate embrace. As I stood before the painting I understood for the first time how love is said to become the space through which everything moves. The love mirrored in her expression contains the full ebb and flow of life, and then exceeds it. All universal experiences seem to rise and dissolve in her, like waves rising and falling on the coast of a hidden cove.

When grief tore the fabric of my own life, this was the love I eventually met. In the early stages of that journey, loss was a spacecraft tearing through a sound barrier I couldn't penetrate on my own. But love carried me past that barrier and revealed life in a completely different light. It showed me that my individual sense of control was an illusion. Love is the only sustaining power.

Love sustained me through the deaths of my dreams and the unimaginable burying of my family. It did not remove my struggles but penetrated them. I kept going only because the howling pain was pierced by the greater force of this resplendent love. Love poured through the opening created by my circumstances until I arrived at a new threshold. I saw a hidden love at the core of life that could not ultimately be defeated. Its presence produced an unexplainable sense of well-being and peace, right in the midst of the chaos. The strength to go on was in its wake.

Unearthing shards of love defined my healing. I learned that darkness and grief are not the final say—they are experiences through which light is not yet visible. But light, in the form of love, is nevertheless there. Nothing exists apart from this numinous presence. We are bathed in love while searching for love. This is the incomprehensible reality of things.

The false or egoic self may be temporarily deceived by heartache, but love is the greater force. Humankind cannot violate this purest love—it can only know it. At every step love asked me to open to a greater vision for my life.

How do we come to realize love? By surrendering to life just as it is. Gradually our eyes open. I think of a good friend who buried her young son. Years later someone asked her if she felt that he had been cheated by life because his years were few. Her response was striking. "I don't think in those terms," she replied thoughtfully. "The answer is that I don't know. I don't know what his life should have been. I realize today that his soul had its own journey and its own terms with life. This had nothing to do with me."

I watched her as she spoke. She was serene and strong. She went on, "But I got to participate for a while in the journey of that soul. For that I am unspeakably grateful."

There was nothing to say in response to her words. The love moving through them was its own flame.

One evening I ate dinner at the home of friends. The aromas from the kitchen were intoxicating and my friend kept checking on things as she continued to prepare our salad dressing. I watched her crush salt and herbs with a pestle. I saw the passion visible on her face every time she opened the oven door. When we finally sat down to eat it was evident that we were eating the love with which she had handled all the ingredients. We were eating the beautiful essence of her being. We were eating her respect for the garden in her backyard and her love for the earth. This is how we come to realize love. We live with our eyes open. We take things in.

In yet another setting, on the occasion of my sixtieth birthday, friends gathered with me for a meal and an evening of celebration. In lieu of gifts I asked them to bring a poem or paragraph that had wakened them at some turning point in their lives. The selections were read by candlelight and were extremely moving. Some friends cried as they read the words they were offering. I thought to myself, this is the way you hope life will be. This is how we come to realize love. We allow our hearts to reach out to other hearts. We draw close.

As we move through our days there is always an option to become the space in which others may recognize love. Sometimes it means giving someone the space they need to think things through—the privacy to arrive at their own conclusions in their own way and to draw conclusions that are different from our own. Or it may mean that I refrain from inserting my own opinions and the force of my rightness. Instead, I observe myself and stop to ask the question, What am I creating in this conversation? Sometimes love calls me to remain silent in order to fully meet someone else and not overwhelm them with my own ideas, or worse, my plan for their life. This is how we come to realize love. We live more carefully. We give each other respect and room to grow. We honor life in every form.

Love is there in the simple, ordinary moments—which in essence are neither simple nor ordinary, because life is not ordinary. The challenge is to see the gift even as we live it and to stop rushing past things. The profusion of buds on my rose bushes, those first signs of spring—the first life since I cut the bushes back in early February—are a perfect expression of the same love. But I have to slow down to know that.

Adversity will be the agent of change in our lives until we decide to let love itself drive the change. Then love, like a mighty tide, will break through the walls that separate us from our inner worlds.

Let go of all that seems to suggest getting somewhere, being someone, having a name and voice, following a policy and directing people in "my" ways. What matters is to love.

—Thomas Merton,
No Man Is an Island

7

An Apparent Detour May Have Unseen Importance

I entered college with the single goal of being a writer. The longing to write professionally had pursued me since my earliest years, and my high school English teacher, Mrs. Allen, fanned that flame. In college the curriculum for English majors began in the sophomore year, and I read and wrote late into the night from September through May. But in the summer before my junior year different realities set in. Did I really think I was going to earn a living writing books? The odds were poor. I needed to find a profession that would pay the bills. I had to be practical. I switched my major in the fall and graduated with a degree in sociology, going right on to pursue graduate studies in counseling/psychology. My focus as well as the heart of my training centered on work with young children.

1970 was a difficult year to find employment in education. Still, after being awarded my Master's Degree, I found a position as a school counselor in an elementary school system in western Massachusetts. Other friends were not as fortunate, and since the course of my own life was set, I offered to drive to Connecticut with a friend while she interviewed for a position as a counselor at an inner-city community college. I even playfully agreed to set up my own interview for the same position, at her request, in order to give her my own perspective. Our drive to Connecticut was filled with laughter about our two interviews, one real, the other in jest.

But as soon as my friend had her own interview with the dean of students she decided that the position was not of interest. Since it was another hour before my own meeting with the dean, she encouraged me to cancel the interview so we could begin the long drive back to New Hampshire. I will never fully understand why I could not agree. I no longer remember. But I kept the appointment.

I was, of course, completely relaxed. There was nothing at stake. I answered all questions with complete honesty and enjoyed the dean of students immensely. I had no prior experience working with drug issues, with different races, or most important, with adults. That the interview even lasted the full hour is, in retrospect, remarkable. Then the unthinkable happened. Right on the spot I was offered the job. The dean of students had a strong intuition that I was the person he'd been searching for. Even less explainable was the fact that everything in me wanted to accept his offer.

I didn't agree to accept the position then and there—I went home and agonized. The fact that I had already signed a contract with a school system in Massachusetts was not something I took lightly. Why was I considering a disruption of my plans in order to accept a position for which I was completely unqualified? If I hadn't driven to Connecticut to keep a friend company this position would never have tempted me. I wouldn't even have known about it. But in the end, I could not fight the strength of my instincts. I accepted the position and moved to Connecticut, immersing myself in a world that became like my second skin. I poured myself into a position for which I seemed to have innate gifts, if not actual credentials.

On the first day of classes, I met a young English professor named Roy D'Arcy. We were married two years later, and the early and tragic deaths of Roy and our first daughter, Sarah, caused me to pick up the pen I had put down twelve years before and write my first book, *Song for Sarah*. The long detour from my original goal, a detour rich in life experience and human suffering, had forced the growth and maturity I needed in order to write meaningfully. The detour that made no sense was actually the preparation I needed to develop as a person. Today I teach aspiring writers that an ease with words is only part of the equation for success in writing. The heart and soul of the writer must also give depth to that facility, or the words have little effect.

What appeared to be a detour was an important leg of my journey . . . even a necessary one. Of course it was almost impossible to see this at the time. Only the clarity of hindsight gave it meaning. I learned that nothing is ever wasted. Every life experience counts because life counts.

In *Outliers*, Malcolm Gladwell reflects that it is often the ability to stick with something that separates those who are successful from those who do not attain their goals. It's not the complexity of the problem that is the stumbling stone—it's feeling discouraged and giving up prematurely. Gladwell describes a study in which students are videotaped while working on math problems. Most of them stick with a difficult homework assignment for only thirty seconds to five minutes. The average is two minutes. Then they give up. But the highest achievers stick with a difficult assignment for twenty minutes. Gladwell's conclusion is clear: Those who excel are the ones who don't quit. They outlast the difficulty. They put one foot in front of the other, even if the meaning of things is not apparent.

Sometimes detours require substantial staying power. Something of great value may be working itself out, but that value may not be immediately obvious or even logical. Still, life is the step we take in this moment. Eckhart Tolle teaches, "There is always only this one step, and so you give it your fullest attention." What appears to be a detour may be vital in the long run. In my own circumstances, moving to Connecticut and accepting that position was life changing. The path contains what you need. A French proverb offers the sentiment, "You often meet your destiny on the road you take to avoid it."

Five years past my losses, but still in the throes of grief and healing, I accepted a job responding to guidance letters for Dr. Norman Vincent Peale's Center in New York. The work was appealing because I was caring for my new daughter and could work from home. I also desperately needed income. It felt that simple. But for the following thirteen years I received so much more than income. I benefited from the education of reading about the lives of people from all over the world through their letters. In retrospect, the opportunity was invaluable. Among its rich gifts was the gift of perspective: I was able to evaluate my own heartache alongside the broken hearts of thousands of others. It was a leveling point.

When Beth entered school I began driving to the Peale Center twice a week. I met other members of the staff and slowly eased my way back into life, but I was still far from the work for which my education had prepared me. At that point Dr. Peale's director of ministry asked me to work as her assistant in the planning of his many retreats and conferences. I initially refused. Learning to design retreats held no interest for me, especially because I couldn't imagine ever needing that knowledge. But the director patiently asked me to reconsider, and I did. I now lead nearly thirty retreats a year, and the knowledge I gained from working at her side has been without equal.

In 2006 my non-profit, Red Bird Foundation, celebrated its fifth year since incorporation. That fall we were asked to offer financial support to a new non-profit in our city, My Healing Place. This vital ministry assists adults, but specifically children, who are grieving. My life had come full circle. Together with Khris Ford, director of My Healing Place, I recently created a video, "Helping Children Grieve," produced by Paraclete Press. In a way I could not have foreseen, I was finally involved with children and healing. Yet none of it had unfolded directly.

The great abolitionist Frederick Douglass said these words in honor of the courageous former slave Harriet Tubman: "The midnight sky and the stars have been witnesses to your devotion to freedom and your heroism. Much of what you've done would seem improbable to those who do not know you."

The truth is that none of us see the path as we walk it, and most journeys seem improbable at times. What appears to be of little account often proves to be of great measure. To know the heart of this world is to traverse the depths of our own hearts. For this to happen we must be led to the people and places that will challenge us. In each circumstance we come face to face with our willingness to stay the course and do the work that our unique life demands. Outward events alone do not shape the inner journey—it is determined by our response to the joys and sorrows we meet on the path. Detours and long delays are the spirit's impeccable guidance. The power of spirit directs us from within.

David Richo tells this story: "In the early 1940's, on the night of her graduation party, a high school girl named Doris Van Kappelhoff was involved in a serious car accident. She had planned to go to Hollywood to become a dancer in films, but her injuries made that future no longer possible. During her long homebound recuperation she began to sing along with the female vocalists on the radio. Her voice became so well trained that she was hired to sing in a band, and soon thereafter, she found parts in movies, changing her name to Doris Day." Her long career as a legendary singer is now well known. Adds Richo, "We are challenged by life's 'mind of its own' to let go of having things come out our way. This is about control . . . and perfect control is the best way to miss out on the joy of life."

Renee La Reau writes, "Often, one seemingly insurmountable obstacle will change the course of your entire life." Adversity moves us from our safe moorings, and positive change results if we agree to be taught by these experiences. Maybe we've been confronted by death, divorce, a move, a loss of job, an illness, years of caretaking, the thwarting of our careful plans . . . At first we sit in the dark and ask: Why has this happened to me? Why is life so unfair? But those questions only lead to deeper cycles of unhappiness and despair; they do not exceed the pain. They contain no power.

There are larger questions: Why am I letting things outside of myself decide whether or not I feel happy and fulfilled? Why am I giving my power away? What if I began to identify with the whole journey, and not just this portion . . . this immediate heartache? What if I recognized, in this detour, this waiting, this particular situation, a summons to fully live my life?

No amount of knowledge prepared me for some of the experiences I have faced: burying my child, living for long stretches with little income while grief tore through me, the experience of utter powerlessness to change circumstances I desperately wanted to change. Some of my detours pounded my life into a different shape. But because of them and the resulting struggle to find my way, I turned toward the spirit that moves through life—and that turning opened doors through which new knowledge entered. I learned that the power had never been in my losses or the obstacles that arise in life, but in the love revealed through them.

Today I see that I had a great investment in the way I pictured life early on—the way I wanted things to go. But life took different turns. Eventually I let go of my insistence that things unfold in a certain way and learned to be deeply grateful for what I had actually been given. In hindsight, this depth of gratitude was precisely what needed to be cultivated in me. The detour had done its work.

Danish philosopher Søren Kierkegaard says, "Every human being comes to earth with sealed orders." His words suggest that every person has a hidden intention for his or her lifetime. If so, then detours steer us toward our necessary events and experiences. But until we can trust the process and receive our lessons consciously, the greater mystery of life does not overtake us, and the detours occur only as stumbling stones that are in our way.

Christian Scripture refers to a time in life when "someone comes and puts a belt around you and takes you where you do not want to go" (John 21). The belt feels like an impediment—an obstacle—a detour from our stated goals and preferred path. But, says Richard Rohr, "The stone brings you down into freedom. It takes you on a different voyage."

The detours—the periods of waiting, the thwarted plans—are teachers for the inner journey. The belt is a disguise, and if we understood that, we'd reach for it and help life put it around our waist. When things come apart and the old images break, when all the things we've never dealt with come to find us, it is to bring about our healing and our deepening. And we must deepen if we are to mature and see what is right before us. Otherwise we stay lost in the small story and believe it to be the sum of life.

Detours have the capacity to "shoot us through the eyes." They teach us how to live in communion with all life—the things we anticipate as well as the surprises. The moment we recognize the detour as a summons from the soul, we're aware of the inner journey, and transformation is possible. Our acquiescence creates the necessary inner shift. It moves attention away from the clamor of circumstances to the world of the inner heart.

While traveling in Lithuania several years ago I was invited to spend a day with an older woman who lived a great distance away. The trip was not part of my original agenda and had nothing to do with the purpose of my visit. It simply arose, and I agreed, even though the time it would take meant that something else would not be experienced.

Her home was humble in every way. She lived fourteen miles from the nearest town, and in an area where it snowed six or seven months of the year, making the streets impassable (except on foot) for that long period. She was in her eighties, living alone much of the time, with no indoor plumbing and a large garden to tend.

Most of her life had been hardship, but her smile held no trace of self-pity or burden. She had no oven, only an open hearth, and in that hearth she had prepared a meal for me and my traveling companions. I watched her. Her hair was white, folded into a bun . . . her dress a deep shade of royal blue, the color of her shining eyes. Midday sun streamed through her windows and a small breeze moved the thin curtains away from the window sill in soft billows. She brought a glass pitcher of apple juice to the table, apples from her tree still floating in the liquid. The juice was warm and delicate. Then, carefully, she placed a china bowl with chicken stew in front of us. The broth was indescribable—I knew it had healing properties.

Parker Palmer speaks of "people who can lead the rest of us to a place of 'hidden wholeness' because they have been there and know the way."

To my physical eyes and measured by Western standards her cottage was barely adequate. And I wouldn't have spent that afternoon in her presence—wouldn't even have met her—but for the change in plans that took us there. Yet that visit has stayed with me and returns to me frequently. It has been a beacon of sorts—a lamp for the journey. A grace. Sometimes all you're given is a brief chance to glimpse the infinite design. John O'Donohue's elegant words return to me: "Every life is braided with luminous moments."

Instead of judging what is, [the wise person] accepts it and so enters into conscious alignment with the higher order. He knows that often it is impossible for the mind to understand what place or purpose a seemingly random event has in the tapestry of the whole. But there are no random events.

—Eckhart Tolle, *A New Earth*

8

*P*ress *On*

*A*fter former slave Harriet Tubman found her way to freedom along the Underground Railroad, she went back to lead hundreds of other slaves to their own freedom in the North. She was tireless, often pushing the limits of human endurance on a path filled with danger. There were huge bounties offered for her capture, and she still pressed on. This was her advice to the frightened slaves who were running toward freedom in the dead of night: "If you hear the dogs, keep going. If you see the torches in the woods, keep going. If they're shouting after you, keep going. Don't ever stop. Keep going. If you want a taste of freedom, keep going." Her words resonate for every circumstance and every age.

The soul's journey in life is demanding. We are called upon to sort through the elements of our lives—our relationships, our heartaches—to find the things that want to be known and the keys that will take us to the right thresholds. Sometimes it's a matter of searching for the one voice, the one person, the one line in a poem. And all along the way we must keep making the choice to move with life, not against it. We learn to let things come and go without demanding that our lives stay the same. We look with newly opened eyes, mindful of our old conditioning and wise to the marketing and advertising that vie for our attention. We look beyond appearances and use our awareness to do something magnificent: We press on.

We begin to accept the nature of life and the human condition. We already know the experience of hope and the experience of defeat. We are familiar with disappointment and disillusionment—the constant stream of life—but we are no longer caught in the drama of each situation. We know there is more. There is a deeper meaning to things and a greater reason for being here. We press on, enjoying the freedom that allows us to see the larger picture. We've turned a corner in the mind and find ourselves in a different place.

What is the path? It is to see past the surface of things—beyond outward appearances. The circumstances of our lives arrive in numerous disguises—poverty, drunk drivers, inflexible systems, unyielding bosses . . . But we press on because now we know these are not our real opponents. Our real opponent is the fear and discouragement that tempts us to stop moving forward—the temptation to quit before new awareness breaks through. Our greatest task is to stand before the circumstances in our lives, just as they are, and meet them—to not turn away. Eventually, through these experiences, we may recognize the spirit moving in life—and understand that it has labored tirelessly on our behalf since our first breath.

"Absorb what comes your way," writes Dan Millman. "Yielding can overcome even a superior force." His words are a reminder. Our power comes from alignment, not resistance. We must move the way life is moving and stop looking back. As we trust our own deepest intuitions, an inner vision becomes our worthy guide.

Press on until you're finally certain that there is no one way life should be. We all made that up. There's only the way life is. Recognizing this, we begin to listen to what life is trying to teach and we stop speeding by, too distracted to ask the questions that will help us find our way: How will I transform my pain? When will I stop racing and notice the world I inhabit—and live in it? How do I reach the deeper part of me? What would open me to a different relationship with life? Why do I resist life's fundamental principles? Suddenly it's clear: I must be willing to let go of my history and ideology—all the details to which I cling—in order to know the spirit in life.

My friend Connie presses forward through life. She has faced health challenges since infancy but possesses an unflagging zest for life and an indefatigable sense of humor. Nothing stops her. She has given birth to children and cared for them against all the odds. She has weathered financial setbacks and multiple moves without a loss in stride. Several years ago she heard about someone who needed a kidney and she said, "I'll do the testing, because that's required as a preliminary step, but I already know that I am a perfect match." She was. And even though agreeing to that surgery put her at risk of worsening her own diminished physical capabilities, she never looked back. "There are times," she said, "when something is so clear to you."

Connie donated the kidney and kept moving forward. Now the recent appearance of cancerous tumors on her liver has slowed her mobility, but not her heart. "This may be it," she said to me. "I'm pretty tired. But oh, it's been good."

In the same breath I think of two young women, dear friends, who both have daughters with serious medical conditions. I watch them from afar. These young mothers are bright, beautiful—engaged and active in every phase of life. They volunteer, they reach out to others, they raise millions of dollars for medical research—and sometimes they sit and cry the tears a mother cries who knows her child may not have a full, long life. They weep from their depths. Then they get up and continue to move forward with the healing work of their own lives and the life of their communities. It is that simple and that difficult. You put one foot in front of the other until the hours of faithful practice bear fruit. Our stories are different, our circumstances are varied, yet the need to find our way remains the same and requires the same dedication.

Years ago while experiencing my first silent retreat, the director told me to spend the first day relaxing. I thought he was wasting my time. Give me something to do, I thought: books to read, things to study. He would not change his assignment and I would not/could not comply.

On the second day his directive was the same. Relax. Slow down. He saw the discipline I lacked and sorely needed: I did not know how to bring my life into balance. Then he added something new: "Take a bubble bath." I left his office fuming. I wanted to learn, to grow. I didn't want to waste time on something frivolous. Third day, the same recommendation. By the fifth day I was worn down. I found some bubbles, poured them into a bathtub and slipped in, still angry. It had taken that long for me to give up my version of things. I only knew how to reach goals and check important items off a list of significant tasks. But he was asking me to transfer my persistence and drive to a completely different set of challenges. In that week I was introduced to the discipline necessary to discover the deeper meaning of things—the foundation stones for a relationship with this beckoning presence. I had to let go of my external drive for outer results and bring that same commitment to the inner journey. I had to learn not to be in charge. I had to learn to listen and to wait.

For so many years I'd been tearing through life with my hyperactive mind and theories, going in many directions at once. Now I was learning to press on with inner work, which would take me to the underglimmer—the work that would make the difference. What the director was really saying to me, although he didn't put it into these words, was: "What do you really want? And how primary are you willing to make this effort? Do you have the staying power to develop new awareness? Can you now develop the necessary discipline?"

"If only we had courage, so much is possible." I knew what was meant when those words were spoken to me, even though, at the time, I was struggling to align their wisdom with my life. So much is possible. But not if we move through life going along instead of living. Not if we are unwilling to pay attention to the lessons life offers or to confront the nature of our everyday choices. Not if we say we are seeking something great but continue to live in a fearful way. Nothing new is possible without following our faith into the full experience of who we truly are. We have to step through the small circles we've drawn around ourselves and become willing to embody the faith that moves mountains. We have to be willing to press on and embody the love about which we speak.

A particular moment in my father's life stands out for me. My mother had suffered a first heart attack at the age of sixty-two and it was fairly serious. The impact of this event on my dad was significant. My mother was the glue in our home. She was the parent who knew the details of our lives. She was the one who called to say, did you get the job? She prepared the family dinners and remembered our birthdays. Our family had a reassuring rhythm because of her presence.

Now she was in cardiac intensive care and I was sitting at the kitchen table with my father, a successful lawyer whose work had always consumed him. He had only danced at the periphery of all our lives. It was my mother who made sure we had a sense of family and solidarity. Now, for the first time, she wasn't there. My father was alone, and the reality sobered him.

I was struck by how fragile he seemed in that moment. The threat of my mother's death wielded a mighty power. All his landscapes were suddenly new, both inner and outer, and his total attention had shifted. He was sitting at that table thinking about things he'd been too busy to consider even a day before, and he was asking questions about life's meaning that he'd never taken the time to ask.

After a long silence he looked at me and said, "Sometimes I wonder what life is really about. What am I doing? How many days have I spent drifting?" He sighed deeply. "I haven't even taken the time to maintain friendships."

It was heartbreaking to witness the fierce clarity of that truth for him, but I didn't say a word, I just sat beside him. I didn't want to get in the way of an inner door that might open for him. I knew that without walking through such doorways we all remain frightened and wander in the ether, never finding our way. We live distracted, in a circle of our own busyness. Yet everything we avoid has the power to bring us down in the end.

For that brief, bright time I hoped my father would be acutely aware of the power of his choices, as well as the tenuous, precious nature of the many things we all take for granted. There's no guarantee we'll be given a tomorrow in which to live differently. All we have is now, and every choice has a consequence.

Wake up! shout the mystics. Don't go back to sleep. The life we're living must become a conscious journey. We must grow increasingly aware of the greater meaning of life and see the sustaining love that not only brings everything into being, but never stops willing the heart to awaken. Waking up isn't a matter of philosophy or theology. We awaken to this ordinary day. We see it. We press on. We put the full force of our resolve behind this quest to see past the surface of things.

Like my father, many experiences in my own life have been the genesis of new sight. But it often happened incrementally—bit by bit I saw things through new eyes. The first time I snorkeled on a coral reef, I was overwhelmed by the sea life just below the surface. The sea was perfectly complete and self-sustaining. I had lived beside the ocean for years and been oblivious to its importance in the circle of life. How many times had I sat at the shoreline and only been vaguely aware of the water's brackish depths? When I finally experienced the great silence beneath the water it was a revelation. The sea was alive and more intimately related to my own life than I had realized. What else was I missing?

No matter how many tries it takes to see through our immediate circumstances, still, love labors on our behalf. Just as I gazed into the sea, we must gaze into life. There is a deeper purpose for being here. Do I have the courage to press on until I can finally stand still and see the design?

Kim Fusco wrote a brilliant first novel, *Tending Grace*. It is a coming-of-age story that reaches into the reader's heart. The central character, Cornelia, is a stutterer. By the end of the story, which is spare and stunning, Cornelia has learned to press on heroically. She finally leans into the shame that arises from her stuttering and also into the painful challenge of her mother's rejection. Ultimately, an elderly aunt helps Cornelia find her authentic self, but not by using words. She accomplishes this by holding a space in which Cornelia is able to come forward; she calls her forth.

Kim's clean and powerful style leaves us, the readers, face to face with our own coming forward. Pressing on, in the end, is always an act of courage.

With a similar devotion, but to an entirely different end, the film *Amazing Grace* tells the story of William Wilberforce, the great anti–slave trade campaigner who fought for twenty years to end the Atlantic slave trade in the British Empire. His turbulent life and career are testament to the seemingly insurmountable obstacles faced by the abolitionists who pressed on without ceasing to change a mind-set and eradicate slavery.

When the change is finally enacted in 1833, Wilberforce is an old man who has achieved a rare feat. But more than his rhetoric, his writings, his tireless parliamentary maneuvers, it is his long dedication to this cause that inspires. What was not thought to be politically possibly becomes, in the end, no match for the fire within. Biographer William Hague concludes, "He set out after his conversion . . . to change the entire moral climate of his country and a good deal of the world." And he did.

There is a quiet light that shines in every heart . . . Without this subtle quickening . . . no horizon would ever awaken our longing . . . This shy inner light is what enables us to recognize and receive our very presence here as blessing . . . Each life is clothed in raiment of spirit that secretly links it to everything else . . . Without warning, thresholds can open directly before our feet. These thresholds are also the shorelines of new worlds.

—John O'Donohue,
To Bless the Space between Us

9

Waking Up to This Day

I awakened recently to learn by e-mail that two friends of mine had died during the same night, thousands of miles apart. Another message in my inbox was from a friend who couldn't sleep during that same night. She wrote about how she had finally gotten out of bed and decided to get some work done, trying to make the midnight hours useful. Someone else wrote that they had arisen before dawn to attend an A.A. meeting. Another woman identified herself just by her first name and her city, and wrote about her continuing heartache because of the death of her son. The next person wrote that she had recently found a beautiful book about hope. Someone else described working the last shift at McDonalds, staying until 2:00 a.m. to clean the greasy ovens.

I myself had sat up late into that same evening, something uncharacteristic of me, in order to watch the documentary film *Promises*. The film is a powerful and troubling portrait of seven Palestinian and Israeli children who live only twenty minutes apart but have completely separate experiences of life.

They are divided by enormous boundaries and grave histories of prejudice and revenge.

The e-mails were a portrait of the day before me and the lives we all live—one life, disguised as completely separate worlds. The voices in my inbox laid out strong images of the human journey, each of us working out the terms of life in our own cities and towns, on our own continents, everyone laboring to find his or her own way. Dan Millman writes, "In an instant a life may turn around—a heart may open in a moment of grace—but preparing for that moment can take a lifetime." He adds, "The mind cannot fathom God. Only the heart. [We are each] only a player in a drama greater than anyone but God can conceive. We can only play the role we are given."

The question is how we will play that role—and whether or not we'll become increasingly aware that there is a new way to be here. It's possible to live from a deeper awareness and to know ourselves as part of something much greater than our individual story.

Last summer I spoke with a man who was one of many hunters dropped off by a small plane on September 9, 2001. The men gathered their gear when the plane landed and waved good bye, eager to set up camp and hunt for three days in a remote spot in the Alaskan wilderness. Then September 11th happened, and no planes could fly for four days to pick them back up. They, of course, had no idea that the world had changed or that anything out of the ordinary had occurred. They had no idea why they'd been left and why no one came for them. News neither penetrated nor affected the woods where they camped. 9/11 had no import there. Something else prevails in the forest.

We need to be willing to know what prevails in the forest, but we have not yet reached that place. Instead we live with a thousand distractions and the belief that something external will make us happy. The place deep inside where our real life goes on is largely unknown. But only in beginning to open to this deeper knowledge will we have the leverage to lift others, and lift this world.

No one says at the beginning, I think I'll refuse to awaken. I'll choose fear, or anger instead. I'll play it small and avoid my life. I'll squander the life I was given. No one decides not to be responsible for the transformation of his or her own pain. But it easily ends up this way. It's subtle. And until we know that our individual growth is linked to the growth of others who inhabit this world, we feel little sense of true responsibility, and our lives consist of an increasing series of small, unconscious choices made over and over again—choices that keep us from deepening.

Viewing earth from space, astronauts and cosmonauts benefit from the actual vision of the Earth as one land, one people, and are radically altered by what their eyes and hearts record. Some are split open by the sight. Yet there are so few of these space travelers to tell us the truth and to counterbalance our large, arrogant presence. Eugene Cernan, watching through the small window of his spacecraft, wrote, "Dawn. Utter darkness. And you don't know where Earth is and something is evoked in you. Something that was already in you. Something that brings you alive."

This something waits for our consent and full attention. It waits for us to recognize what we're doing to one another— waits for us to feel our real connection not only to those in our own neighborhoods and families, but those who work in rice fields and groves of olives half a world away. It waits for us to recognize within creation the reflection of our own soul and to know that we are more, not less, than the systems and goods we accumulate in order to convince ourselves that life has meaning. There's more than the surface of things. It is a true relationship with the underglimmer that we are lacking.

One morning when I was writing in Alaska, I watched the early light open the day. A small boat pulled into the cove in front of my cabin. No motor. It moved effortlessly on the water. I put down my journal and watched more closely.

It was a line of light, approaching the cove like a water bird. A fishing line hung off the back of the boat. There was a sudden, imperceptible tug on the line, but only that. The boat continued to shimmer on the water, both of them, boat and water, different openings to the same wideness.

What if we weren't held so tightly in the grip of our beliefs and points of view? What if we were free of the mind-sets they create? What if we knew ourselves to be this wideness? Who or what will loosen our moorings and topple us, helping us to know? Who will help us recognize the consciousness that is laboring to awaken humankind. We are one spirit, one heart.

Another small boat, *The Alpine Lady*, chugged past heading for open waters, perhaps in search of halibut or king salmon.

As she moved past, her motor was a small whine that broke the morning quiet. I followed her and the current, first with my eyes, and then with my complete attention. The water drew me in. Spirit is like a ship cutting through the channel, making room for what was meant to be.

Months before our first international conference for women, WOMENSPEAK 2007, became a reality, a team of women began to shape it by the simple act of paying attention to their own lives. We lived with this question: Am I able to see myself as someone tending the emergence of something beautiful? Few days passed without one of us finding and sending a poem or simple words of encouragement to the others. Author Jean Shinoda Bolen writes, "The outer world numbs us to what soul has to say . . . You are carrying the seeds of something that will change your life and the world."

But juggling so many things, who stoops down to water small seeds? Who notices all that connects humankind, and the beauty and purpose of the Earth? Yet everything depends on whether or not we have the will to see directly, and then to love what must be loved.

While in Alaska, my small cabin in Kachemak Bay was at the retreat center Stillpoint Lodge. The irony of my cabin's name was not lost on me: *Point of View.* The space was small, perfect. The glass sliding doors at the end of the bed were a port of entry, opening the little world of my cabin to the bay and the mountains, to wildlife . . . to the watchful moon. To the same waters that took me to the whales.

Tucked beside the head of my bed was a closet with a compost toilet. Next to the east window was a sink whose "running" water was a jug positioned above the sink and then upended into a porcelain base, creating a miniature water cooler. There were no pipes. A small bucket in the cabinet beneath the sink had to be emptied when it grew too full. A desk, an oversized chair, a good bed quilt. Then a quick walk to the main house past bouquets of brilliantly colored lady slippers in the organic garden for a hot shower. This was it—paradise outside my door.

At first it was difficult to settle down and write. I spread my journals and books in stacks underneath the desk and littered the bed quilt with papers and a quilted case with pens and highlighters. But the call of the wild just beyond the door was palpable. Everything there shot me through the eyes. It was painfully clear, watching the fluctuating tides and sensing the glacier just over the rise, that life in its full magnificence is meant to be known. The Universe without mirrors the universe within. "How will you say thank you and have a relationship with these foundations of life?" ask the elders.

One evening it rained through the night, hard and pelting, and the next morning the mountain tops were white. The natives call it termination dust—the covering that marks the end of summer and the beginning of the long dark. I sat on my deck watching the small portion of the cove that was visible from that position. Mountains, water, water life. The weather changing continuously—hourly. That morning the tide was out and there was no way to put a skiff in the water and leave, no matter how urgent your business. There was only the grainy swell of the sandbar.

Gulls and loons inched their way along the edge of the shore picking at insects and small marine life. Wooly, rounded heads of sea otters bobbed in the distance. An eagle circled the mountains, her head a heart-stopping spot of gold light as the sun broke through the clouds and fell on her white crown. The air was still full of moisture from the rain. Water clung to the pine trees in small droplets—rows and rows of them. Small sacs of life.

I walked slowly to the lodge kitchen. Wellyngton, the cook, had left my breakfast bowl on the counter. I layered it with his granola and cooked grains, topping it with a blueberry/raspberry compote made from berries picked on the island. Ordinary elements of life, yet the taste indescribable. I was hungry and yet felt full after three or four mouthfuls, the porridge being so much more than a simple meal.

Wellyngton is originally from Brazil. I kept urging him to reveal to me his magic with food, as if he could. All his offerings were ineffable, every flavor and bite an amazement. He seemed to hear the earth speaking in its own voice and be capable of translating that sound into a meal of great subtlety. "You have to put worries aside and approach food respectfully," he finally offered. "Engage it."

One morning I watched as he spread dozens of ingredients across the counter. He considered each of them for hours, taking into account flavor, aroma and the way each element would support other ingredients in the dish. "I cook because I love," he finally said. He shrugged and smiled shyly. What else to say? He returned to his alchemy and I to my writing.

White gulls streamed through the air, the moon's great pull from the night before already relaxing. The water was now slowly slipping back to shore, its cycle fulfilled. I sat cross-legged, cradling the small white breakfast bowl and silver spoon between my knees. The berries and grains temporarily removed the illusory distance between the mountains and the eagle, and between both of them and me—the one watching. Everything in sight burst with vital energy: each living creature, the land formations, every crawling insect, every cloud. All around me countless expressions of a single force of life—and in that rare moment, my thoughts were no longer interpreting what was before me. There was only life, just as it is.

In her journal, *Locked Rooms and Open Doors*, Anne Morrow Lindbergh writes, "Who is not afraid of pure space—the breathtaking empty space of an open door?"

One night in Alaska I was invited to go raspberry picking with Don, a longtime sailor who now lives on a houseboat in the middle of the cove. A porthole from his last ship is set inside one of the doors to his house and the glass reflects the surrounding water and sky. We walked from the houseboat down several sections of dock, across a plank or two, right onto the isthmus. From there we followed a stretch of dirt road to the patch of berries. The thick bushes and scratchy leaves reached high above my head.

Don gave me a plastic bucket through which he'd threaded a thin black cord. I hung the cord around my neck and got to work. There we were, our fingers stained red, threading our way through the bushes. I'd accepted the invitation because I was intrigued by someone who chose to live in such a remote spot, floating on water. A couple of times we stepped away from the thicket of berry leaves to talk face to face, but most of our conversation floated up from the tangle of dense growth, interrupted a few times by the antics of his new kitten.

Later that evening we sat on the houseboat talking, eating fish, and drinking homemade ginger ale. Don spoke a lot about the sea. It was raining when he brought me back to the dock near my cabin and by the time we arrived, my hair was dripping wet. He'd guided the skiff over the water and through the rain in the dark of night without a headlight. He knew the water. He felt it. We glided across the cove in silence.

"Want what you already hold," writes Mary Anne Radmacher.

What am I holding? Ordinary things. Fresh raspberries. A glimpse of life on a houseboat in a wild land. A dinner plate of cod, salad greens, and tomatoes grown and ripened in a houseboat window. The flight of a blue heron. Daily mist lifting and falling on the mountains. Conversations about the pull of the tide and how the half moon is considered an auspicious time for travel. This is what I'm holding: life. This day.

Everyone works out his or her own way and follows a unique path. We make the choices we're conscious enough to make. All the while, knowledge of the deeper nature of things is here. Creation is here, its voice, at the core of us, expressing a certain radiance. When we're willing to know life directly, we see the pristine depth that surrounds us. Then we see that this same depth *is* us. "Within" and "without" are concepts of the mind.

What am I doing with this brief experience of life? The question fills the hours. We live and work consumed by details and the meaning we've assigned to those details, until we finally convince ourselves that the mystery of being here is within our control. We're susceptible to so many lies and see dimly, at best. We notice the seasons and experience weather patterns. We comment on how these occurrences impact our plans—the ten thousand things. How will this downpour affect my morning commute? But we have yet to know rain or snow, really. We watch them without seeing.

Even so, the cycle of life continues to re-create itself before us. Energy explodes in the swelling tides and the long veils covering the mountain peaks. Day after day Nature surrenders one form of herself so that other species and creations can flourish. The life-life cycle. Everything straining to support this Eden. Everything ready to evoke that which is already embedded within life, bringing it alive. Everything waiting for a door to open, a veil to lift, waiting for us to respond to the "breath-taking empty space."

The glaring light that breaks through the Alaskan sky is the same light that warms the sheets and laundry I hang on my makeshift, backyard clothesline at home, thousands of miles away. Stringing the rope and wrapping it around the posts of my weathered fence was a small ritual, a reclaiming of something lost. The first night I lay down on the sheets I had hung outside to dry was notable. The smell of fresh cotton brought back childhood years when lying down each night on sun-dried linens was routine.

One light illuminates the cosmos. One light passes over the cities and stretches in long columns across the steel buildings, reflected by the squares of glass. One light finds its way through the towering pines in the deepest forests, awakening plants and mosses that grow far from human sight. One light moves in the depths of the waters.

And even though it is paradoxical to the mind, each seemingly separate expression of life manifests this one light. The air and the soil beneath our feet are the same single force. We do not exist apart from any of this. Within us it exists as our inner nature; outside of us, as the Universe. Perhaps sleeping on the wind is one step closer to knowing.

Denise Roy drives her five-year-old daughter, Julianna, to school one morning and records their conversation in her book, *My Monastery Is a Mini Van.*

"Mama?"

"What sweetie?"

"The whole world is inside of you. And inside of me."

My friend Craig responds to the light by composing music. He hears harmonies that escape most ears and masterfully stretches them from the rivers and seas—draws them across ravines and remote forests—pulls them tenderly though beds of flowers and hidden meadows, through skyscrapers and across speedways. As a last movement he threads them through the voices of his choir. The local paper likens listening to his music to "rolling on a great sea."

In a sense Craig, the musician, and Wellyngton, the cook, are kindred spirits. They unveil the present day, bringing it momentarily within reach. See, here it is. Listen. Taste.

Night skies in Alaska blaze with light, especially in places far from the city. I trace Orion's belt with my finger. I follow the brightness from Venus across the water as she casts a liquid path of skylight along the line already hurled through space by the moon. When I rise early in the morning, the glittering stream is still there. Every morning we decide what we will tend that day. We decide what we can bear to know, or see.

The mountaintops in Alaska are often veiled by cloud, but one evening, just before a rain, the night was unparalleled. I stood alone on the path to my cabin, a full moon pouring over the water, pink streams of light shadowing its reflection in the surrounding sky. I stood there watching, breathing—standing before the depth and radiance of the life force shining down through the moonlight. The night air was cold, the mountain peaks already wet with snow. I thought of the Neil Diamond song "Be," and how one word could encompass this night and the privilege of being here to see it. One word to capture being alive.

That afternoon I'd been on a high point above the cove looking at rocks with long, thin lines scratched on their faces where the glacier scraped across their surface. The view from this height was panoramic, but more than that, it was the light. Light on aspen trees, their leaves already turning. Light on the forest. Light on water. Wild, velvety light. A twenty-foot-deep artesian spring lay there, but to the naked eye it looked like a shallow, glittering pond. Small song birds in the grasses. In every direction—toward the mountains, the glacier, the open ocean, the forest—energy in the form of light.

With your back against the glacial rock, eyes blinded by the light of brilliant white gulls in flight, you realize that if you are not aware enough of life to notice this day, you are taking up too much space here. You're not living to the greatness that calls us forth. Awakening to this day and seeing its inherent beauty is the mastery. It is all sacred. All miracle.

The light demands that I let interpretations and symbols go, and pushes me to the place where it is only me and the night and the fierce dark—only this brief lifetime and the cresting of the moon. Only this moment that holds the first light of day. Then I say, with Gerald May, "I want to be taken in."

In the book *Home Planet*, cosmonaut Vladimir Shatalov reports that "there is always a storm happening somewhere. Lightning flashes sometimes cover up to a fourth of the continent—a majestic spectacle. [Yet] aboard the spacecraft it's quiet. Peals of thunder can't be heard. Gusts of wind can't be felt. It seems as if everything is calm, and you're watching a play of light."

❧

Alaska still has the allure of wild, untamed land. The routines of city life are far removed. The small coves and glacial rises demand presence. Even the thirteen hours of travel it takes to get to this cove creates a great divide. Two commercial air flights, a ride on a small plane, a ferry—just to arrive. When you step off the ferry you've already crossed a threshold.

From this vantage point the relative length of a human life span seems surprisingly brief. Trivialities are unmasked when the chores of day-to-day living require such effort. Here it is obvious that most concerns simply don't matter. You stop being fooled.

"From space," say the astronauts, "there's a silence the depth of which you've never experienced before. And you think about what you're experiencing, and why . . . and it comes through to you so powerfully. You look down and see the surface of that globe that you've lived on all this time, and you know all those people down there, and they are like you. They are you. And somehow you recognize that you're a piece of this total life" (Russell Schweickart, *Home Planet*).

❧

In *The Year of Magical Thinking*, Joan Didion looks back on the day preceding the sudden death of her husband. She muses that at one point he had twenty-four hours left to live but didn't know it. That single thought threads through her story like a mantra. She repeats it often, reliving over and over the sudden shock of his limited hours. "How would he have chosen to live those [last] hours," she wonders, "if he had known how few hours were left?"

This same question pushes against our unexamined beliefs and rises up inside our dreams. It arrives disguised as restlessness, discontent, emptiness—the longing that will not let us go. And always, an arm's length away, the "breath-taking empty space."

How would I choose to live my last hours if I knew in advance? How am I choosing to live this hour? The present moment presses in from all sides. This day breathes into us like a bellows, working to fan fear and lethargy into sight.

My friend Susan says, "We *are* earth, and she is us. She is power, mystery—life force. Everything we do impacts everything else. The energy of our choices moves throughout the world."

Once, driving in a large city I saw a roughed-up man shuffling slowly through the grass and stubble at the highway's edge. His grey hair was thick and matted. I noticed that his hands were trembling. He was working the light at this particular highway intersection, carrying a sign made with cheap cardboard and a black sharpie. The sign read, I'M HUNGRY. He stared into the SUVs and pickups as they passed, searching with his eyes. PLEASE.

In *Home Planet*, cosmonaut Oleg Makarov reflects on his orbit in outer space. "Within seconds of attaining orbit around the Earth, all uttered a confused expression of delight and wonder. The sight of Earth from space was breathtaking—

incomparable. Something about the unexpectedness of the sight and its incompatibility with anything we've ever seen or experienced on Earth, with anything we've known or practiced. Involuntarily it elicits a deep, emotional response, this spectacle of our small planet haloed in blue."

PLEASE.

"The flapping of a single wing reverberates to make a tiny change in the atmosphere," says Susan. "That change could cause little things that can have big effects." Like the clarity of looking at the world and others from an inner place, finally recognizing who we are and how much is possible.

The man at the intersection is dirty, sunburned, his dank shirt falling in loose wrinkles around his thin frame. No one cranks a window, but he seems unaffected. He is restless and walks back and forth, up and down, just like we do.

Immaculee Ilibagiza speaks about the killing fields she experienced in Rwanda. "In the midst of genocide," she says, "I heard something. And I saw that there is a huge world inside of us."

I heard something.

Please, says the man carrying the homemade sign.

Every small decision has a cumulative effect.

How would he have chosen to live if he'd known how few hours were left? writes Didion.

How did the whales hear our silent call to them, asking them to come?

What am I willing to know in order to change my life?

We could live in a different way. We could deepen.

We could bring the power that lies within us to bear on life, if we had the courage to know it ourselves.

Do I have the courage it takes to awaken?

We don't have to repeat an endless stream of choices based on fear.

"We separate spirit and matter as if they were two different things," writes Joan Chittister. "We are, all of us, swimming in an energy that is God."

During my last week in Alaska I stood at the sliding glass door in my cabin and scanned the muddy shoreline at low tide. I memorized the clouds overhead and the magpie or two sitting on the deck railing. But after a brief return to my writing, when I looked up again, the view before me was new. Everything had changed within minutes, even if imperceptibly.

It reminded me of how I once experimented with change when I took a painting class with artist Mary Southard. I began by using my non-dominant left hand, making broad purple brush strokes across the page. I wanted to feel what the brush would do—could do. I was exploring color. For a while I played with the splotches of paint that dropped when I used a smaller brush. I liked the freedom of not caring where the paint was going. I liked it when the crimson shades took the lead. I liked it that nothing stayed the same.

The night I picked raspberries and had dinner on the house-boat I met Don's four-month-old kitten, Cleo. She is a master of change. She's soft and sleek with a creamy white fur ruffled with long thin streaks of grey. She had already fallen off the houseboat dock into the frigid Alaska water two or three times. It happened again the evening I was there for dinner. She appeared at the door soaking wet on her bottom half. Something intrigued her and she ventured right over the edge.

It was the same in the painting studio. You just keep applying splotches of color until one of them becomes something, and you venture over the edge and follow it into life. Philip Simmons, just before dying young from ALS, wrote that "to see the world through a lover's eyes is already to have chosen it." He knew. You fall in, like the kitten. You fall, like the splotches of color. You summon a deeper courage and wade into the water. You make choices.

I think about choosing love, especially as it heaves through the terrible darkness that sometimes envelops us—choosing to live dangerously like a kitten, pattering feet rushing to explore, then plunging bottom first into the brine. Or clouds moving across the heavens, forming patterns that split apart then float together again. Choosing to see an iris, just as it is. Choosing to know what really matters. Putting down ideologies and theories and just looking . . . seeing what's there. Letting in the day.

It's a large commitment to play the hand life has dealt us, and it takes courage to make unbounded brush strokes with our lives—living into ordinary moments that turn us upside down. But one day you simply agree to the terms of life, the movement and change, all the impermanence, and the absolute stillness underneath.

You finally understand that there's no way anything was supposed to be. You see a patch of raspberries and a palette of paint. You've felt the movement of love in darkness, and the movement of love in light. You observe that everything is basically unknown and realize the terrible effort it takes to press on and see through even one disguise. But you do. You shift the pivot of your existence from outside to inside—from the surface to the depth within.

A seagull honks into the morning, its wing pulled flat and taut against the thermals. Resilient, radiant in flight, it soars above the water. Other gulls join and form a long V. They move perfectly, the same mind, one mind—intrinsic and self-directed—as we might be. Whether I am in Alaska or walking city streets, life rises up.

Before leaving Alaska I follow the steep, rocky climb to a nearby glacier with two friends. We climb for an hour, finally reaching the flat known as the saddle, and stop to smell the primeval forest. Wild cranberries, tart and chewy, fill the bushes close to the trail. We resume walking at a steady pace over a rock field, the glacier no more than a few hundred feet away.

We turn one more corner and I see elegant formations of blue white ice floating in the water. Just at that moment a loon cries. Behind the floating ice sculptures is the glacial mass. I barely take it in. Gerald May once described the cry of a loon as "the sharp cry of being alive." He added, "Something distinctly human in me, something civilized, keeps my cry inside."

Theologian Howard Thurman writes, "Something within each of us waits and listens for the sound of the genuine. If you hear it and turn away, your life will be crippled. If you hear it and turn toward it, it will free you."

Life will either be lived, or we will "go along."

Once, driving east from Yosemite Falls with my daughter Beth, it felt as if the land was physically taking us in . . . as if we were driving into "middle-earth" with its rushing brooks and lakes, sequoias lining the road. The following day, at Death Valley, the temperature was 118 degrees. The car overheated, and we drove without air conditioning for five hours. We were soaked with sweat, the salt dunes baked in heat. When we stopped driving there was total silence. Complete, absolute silence. Not another soul around. And then, a hum. Earth. The sound of energy. The sound of the life force, the sound of this day.

We inched along to Badwater, the lowest elevation in the Western Hemisphere. The wind was a blast of fire on our faces and arms and we were instantly tanned. I tried to wash the car windshield and the water evaporated with a sizzle the second it touched the glass. Everything was burning up. We waited. And then, at the end of that very long day, a full rainbow appeared with both the setting sun and a bolt of lightning within its arch.

How to grasp this unfolding power and its effortless beauty? How to live within the miracle? David Whyte writes about a drawing tide whose pull is so strong we cannot believe it is meant for us. But that's precisely it. The drawing tide is meant for us.

Now you're no longer inside something with a window looking out at a picture. Now you're out there and there are no frames, there are no limits, there are no boundaries. You're really out there, going 17,000 miles an hour, ripping through space, a vacuum. And there's not a sound. There's a silence the depth of which you've never experienced before . . .

Are you separated out to be touched by God, to have some special experience that others cannot have? And you know the answer to that is no. There's nothing you've done to deserve this, to earn this; it's not a special thing for you. You know very well at that moment, and it comes through to you so powerfully, that you're the sensing element for man.

—Russell Schweickart, *Home Planet*

Epilogue

The seed of this book was sown in a talk I gave at a conference in California several years ago. I thought it would be fairly simple to re-create the talk on paper, as the publisher requested, but nothing has been further from the truth. The work has had its own life, demanding that I listen with care, moment by moment, to what wanted to be said. It has also called me to remain faithful to the beating of my own heart.

Author Joko Beck writes, "Our function is not to live forever, but to live this moment." I always marvel when one simple sentence seems to summarize the heart of everything you are reaching for. Waking up to this day is, in fact, my ongoing practice—but it is not always easy. That's why the days I spent in Alaska became so rich. When daily demands are momentarily put aside, it is easier to find the openings. Nature continues to be my guide. Periodically stepping away from daily routines no longer seems a luxury, but a necessity.

During the months of writing I pored through the writings offered by astronauts and cosmonauts as they left not only the daily routine, but the earth's orbit, and looked back at this planet from space. Their reflections offer an enormous perspective. Eugene Cernan observed, "There is only light if sunlight has something to shine on. When the sun shines through space it's black . . . the light must have something to strike." So I offer this work as something for the light to strike.

As I finish writing there has been a strong Texas hail storm. It reminds me of a night when I lived in a smaller Texas town, semi-secluded, on the top of a rise. That property was hit by lightning several times. One memorable evening I sat on my couch in the dark, swiveling my head to follow the lightning strikes. I was scared silly, and yet, at the same time the storm, like the soul's journey, was lovely beyond description. I notice that those two things often go together: our sheer fright and a peerless beauty.

We are the night ocean filled with glints of light. We are the space between the fish and the moon, while we sit here together.

—Rumi, *A Year with Rumi,*
January 12th Reading

About the Author

*P*aula D'Arcy, a writer, retreat leader, and conference and seminar speaker, travels widely in the United States, Canada, and abroad. She is president of the Red Bird Foundation, which supports the growth and spiritual development of those in need and furthers a ministry both to those in prison and those living in third world or disadvantaged cultures.

Paula's ministry grew from personal tragedy. In 1975 she survived a drunk-driving accident that took the lives of her husband and twenty-one-month-old daughter. Pregnant at the time, Paula survived the accident to give birth to a second daughter, Beth Starr. She tells her story in two bestselling books, *Song for Sarah* and *Gift of the Red Bird*.

A former psychotherapist who ministered to those facing issues of grief and loss, Paula worked with the Peale Foundation, founded by Dr. Norman Vincent Peale, from 1980 until his death in 1993. Today her work includes leading workshops and retreats related to spirituality, aspiring writers, and women's gatherings, including Women's Initiation and Rites of Passage. In recent years she has teamed with Richard Rohr to present seminars on the Male/Female Journey and Spirituality in the Two Halves of Life.